Pam
Little

Mystic Grits

Mystic Grits

A Southern Girl's Journey to Wisdom

Darelyn **DJ** Mitsch

PYRAMIS PRESS

PUBLISHED BY PYRAMIS PRESS

FIRST EDITION

Designed by Brian M Johnson & N Silas Munro, LOUDEST ink LLC
Illustrations by Carolyn Butler

ISBN 10: 0-615-30087-1
ISBN 13: 978-0-615-30087-0

TABLE *of* CONTENTS

□ ◇ □ ◇ □ ◇ □ ◇ □ ◇ □ ◇ □ ◇ □ ◇ □ ◇ □ ◇ □ ◇ □ ◇ □ ◇ □ ◇ □ ◇ □ ◇ □

TABLE *of* CONTENTS

□ ◇ □ ◇ □ ◇ □ ◇ □ ◇ □ ◇ □ ◇ □ ◇ □ ◇ □ ◇ □ ◇ □ ◇ □ ◇ □ ◇ □ ◇ □ ◇ □ ◇ □ ◇ □

TABLE *of* CONTENTS

□ ◊ □ ◊ □ ◊ □ ◊ □ ◊ □ ◊ □ ◊ □ ◊ □ ◊ □ ◊ □ ◊ □ ◊ □ ◊ □ ◊ □ ◊ □ ◊ □ ◊ □ ◊ □

TABLE of CONTENTS

¤ ◊ ¤ ◊ ¤ ◊ ¤ ◊ ¤ ◊ ¤ ◊ ¤ ◊ ¤ ◊ ¤ ◊ ¤ ◊ ¤ ◊ ¤ ◊ ¤ ◊ ¤ ◊ ¤ ◊ ¤ ◊ ¤ ◊ ¤

"It is the modern mystic who will lead the way. What's possible is remembering who we really are and living in a more conscious space, we can stand fully in the understanding that what we do affects everyone and everything. It is only with that conscious awareness of our interconnectedness that the world we all hope for can result.

The modern mystic is integrated—the worldly self and the spiritual self working as one. The modern mystic is you."

LAURA BERMAN FORTGANG
The Little Book on Meaning

□ ◇ □ ◇ □ ◇ □ ◇ □ ◇ □ ◇ □ ◇ □ ◇ □ ◇ □ ◇ □ ◇ □ ◇ □ ◇ □ ◇ □ ◇ □ ◇ □ ◇ □ ◇ □

Prologue

January 24th, 2008

I came into my office today and found this note from Bev:

> *"To put in my small 2 cents – I understand you're working on
> the other business book and getting that to market as soon as
> possible; from a monetary and competitive standpoint, that
> more than makes sense. But deep, deep in my heart, I hope you
> do not put your GRITS on the back burner. You have had this
> in your heart for soooo long and now that the memories and
> thoughts are coming back to life to be shared with people like*

*me, please don't stop. Okay, maybe I am selfish in that I want
this book to help me on my own journey. Because I know you?
Maybe. Because it is something I am searching for? Maybe. But I
think NOT! Your book reflects who you are – creative, fun, emotional, and intelligent, with a touch of Sass! GRITS! Many of us
are waiting.*

Don't stop. Don't stop. Don't stop!"

Bev

Bev is the soft–spoken, platinum blonde executive assistant
who had retired to North Carolina with her husband two years
earlier. She had thankfully landed in the part-time role of managing my brain and my calendar in our corporate coaching company.
I dropped into my cushy leather chair and grabbed my chest with
my right hand to keep my heart from falling out.

She was right. Mystic Grits was calling to me with such force
I could no longer ignore it. I had started and stopped writing this
book since the fall of 2000. My gal pals had grown weary of asking about it. Every time I set the writing aside I thought to myself,
"I will just wait and come out of this spiritual closet later when I am
an old woman and nobody in my home town cares too much about
me or what I might say."

Well, Welcome really isn't a town; it's an unincorporated community. I left it behind along with a handful of friends, some
divorce guilt and a boatload of family in 1979, when there were
only 1,900 people and a sign that read "Welcome to Welcome,
a Friendly Place." Now there are 30,000 people, and most of
the newcomers had never heard about Welcome or seen it on
a map until they drove through on their way to somewhere else.
Apparently they stopped to see Dale Earnhardt's cars in the Richard
Childress Racing Museum and ended up staying for the Bar-B-Que

and hush puppies. But those I left behind are still very much a part of my fabric and I was afraid if they ever discovered some of my secrets – my magical stories or dream interpretations– I might not be able to "go home again."

As I resisted writing this, I realized it was confronting just how much of who I am is still stuck there in the 60s and 70s somewhere among the LPs, ironed hair, loud mufflers, Christmas Cantatas and altar calls. I also realized I have lived a lifetime of paradox – on one hand, I was the church lady who was faithful in attendance and, on the other, I was inquisitive and constantly seeking answers beyond what I was taught as a child. I learned to step out on the faith that the folks I most loved would see the humor, the questions, and my experiences as entertainment if nothing else, for I revere the love and care in which I was raised to become a storyteller and seeker. This was a new type of faith for me—not the standard Bible story kind, but the type of faith I had to find in trusting myself.

So I went home on that January day after reading Bev's note and quietly asked my mind's little voice of judgment and limitations to 'shut up' for a few minutes while I looked around for something. I climbed the ladder to my attic to collect dust-covered journals and diaries among the luggage, my kid's outgrown clothes, and that vast collection of Beanie Babies I thought would make me rich one day. I wanted to see if there was a story worth reading in the diary pages written as I explored the depths of my soul during life transitions and spirit-filled growth spurts. Pulling from these journals just a few of the cosmic events and deeper inquiries that have fueled my spiritual journey, I have pieced together a sampling of stories from a "girl raised in the south" – or as Fannie Flagg called us, "GRITS."[1] I selected some of the journal entries in a rather random order, but when we paged through them, they were organized in small books representing four distinct phases of my life.

And, of course, there is that buffet sampling of soul food that always finds a way into my writing, popping up here and there.

Much of what I included is true, though I allowed myself some creative license and wrote this as meta-fiction. In doing this I changed the names of people I wanted you to know, those who helped shaped me but who were best left as alias characters. Others allowed me to use their real names, for which I am grateful. Each of these souls is a gift to me even those who don't appear that way. I have learned so much from those who have graced me with their friendship, their patience, their love, their challenges, and even their anger.

Eight months and 1,400 pages later I sat cross-legged on the floor of my piano room with an earth angel who pulled sections from the three different versions of the book I'd written in less than a year. Still starting and stopping, writing and editing, I was at a loss for what to include in a format someone would take time to read. I had written the equivalent of War and Peace, which was not something I'd intended to do.

Then I realized that those stories we selected in a rather random way were the real diary and journal entries. These best tell my story. The expressions of dreams interpreted, of healing, of introductions to worlds beyond this one, of what it means to learn from our children, and of the longings for meaning at midlife have all found a place here. In reflection of what is now within, I have also found there was probably something worth sharing and hopefully something worth reading, at least for my dear Bev.

PROLOGUE

BOOK I
FOUNDATIONS

My view now about
Foundations of Faith

From family traditions and beliefs to the kitchen table wisdom of our grandmothers, I have found that it is our myths, stories, and beliefs that shape us. These hand-me-down ideals set us on a path to live as mere interpretations of ancestral beliefs or to ask deeper questions, seeking and finding meaning by observing and questioning the world around us—learning truths from our own spiritual quest and evolution.

I have learned that our foundations give us a framework for exploration, the best questions we can ask. It is in learning to ask powerful questions about who we are and what we are doing that we access our own best answers—our wisdom. We may have a collective epiphany and simply realize that we arrive naked and alone on this planet and typically leave that same way. It's what happens in the middle, between our arrival and departure—the people we attract and build relationships with, the circumstances we manage, the gifts we contribute, the potential for learning—that makes it worth the effort of being born.

It was my confusion about some of my early Bible teachings that set me on a path of discovery about such things when I was young. I asked too many questions. I wondered why we said the Apostle's Creed at my church, (I believe in God the Father, I believe in the Holy Spirit, the Holy Catholic Church, etc.) and yet we were told that Catholics weren't going to be going to heaven with us Baptists because they hadn't been saved. If that was true, why did we acknowledge the Catholics in our creed, I wondered? I heard pastors teach against Catholicism and it bothered me for several reasons, primarily for how wrong it seemed that we could be the judge of who went to heaven, or not. I also wondered about Jesus being King of the Jews, but it was us Protestants that worshipped him. I couldn't make sense of why Jewish people didn't recognize him as the Messiah if they had really waited all those years for the fulfillment of the prophecies.

I wondered if Jesus got into trouble when he was ten or eleven, or like most teenagers, did he live under the threat that he might have a "knot jerked in his tail" if he ever questioned authority? What happened if he practiced magic or read the Ouija Board?

I had a hunch that Mary Magdalene hung out for more than feet washing, but then I was taught that Jesus didn't hang out with girls. Then I was confused about how he turned water into wine at a wedding—his first recorded miracle—and why we weren't supposed to drink wine, even at weddings. I figured turning water into grape juice would be cool too, but that didn't seem to have the same punch in a miracle story as instant fermentation. I just had a ton of questions. (Don't get me wrong. I was then and am still crazy about God and Jesus, but that's not the point, and it isn't what this work is about.)

Even as a teenager I wondered who decided about which books to keep in the Bible and which ones to delete. I was curious. I never felt lost, but it seemed most people I knew wanted to make sure I was saved over and over again. I got the notion that I needed to be protected from myself and my sins, and I must have had a bunch of those given how guilty I felt most of the time about the things I thought about—especially, well, you know—sex. So I would go to the altar often, sometimes feeling really moved by the Spirit and confessing my sins (which I heard was the same thing the Catholics did when they went to confession in a booth), and sometimes by the time I got to the front of the church, I had to make something up to be forgiven for because for the life of me, there were times I couldn't remember why I was there.

This confusion and these questions started when I was a child. And I would often find peace in my prayers and in my dreams—but the best answers came directly from my conversations with Maw Maw Precious.

Magic

If you ever have the notion to search your attic for the diaries of your youth—the journals that kept your heart under lock and key, those sacred places that held your most intimate thoughts—go back and find them. Search and find the reminders and memories and recreate your story. These thoughts and longings helped give you life and set you on the journey you've traveled. And if you are searching for what's next, these memories may hold the key for what you were born to do.

Come with me to my attic and I will share with you what I've found. It is my wish that as you read my story, you will find permission to share your own.

June 11, 1965

Dear Diary,

Today is my 10th birthday and I got this diary as a present from my cousin Kathy. After I opened my presents, Kathy and I played with the Ouija Board I got for Christmas. It spelled out Paul McCartney as the Beatle I love most. It's true! I love Paul, and I have all his bubblegum trading cards.

When the triangle moves to the letters on the Ouija Board, I feel buzzing under my hands. It lifted right off the board when we asked what I will be when I grow up! It spelled T-E-A-C-H-E-R. Yuck! That's not what I want to be. I want to be an airline stewardess and see the whole wide world.

I have to tell Maw Maw Precious about the Ouija Board. She likes to talk about my magic.

Your friend,

Precious Darelyn Darr

Funny, I always signed my diary with my full name, as if to confirm that I had a relationship with my secret book. As I read this first page, an essence of me at ten years old washed over me, and all my senses were transported back in time. I closed my eyes and could see Maw Maw Precious with her long black-and-silver braids wrapped around her head in circles and pinned into a hair hat. I used to see light around her hair hat – white, yellow, and blue light– glowing in big halos as she danced from chore to chore around the farm, milking the cows, stirring laundry in the large tubs in the wash house, or cooking the most amazing meals for our large family and friends three times a day.

I think it might be the smell of Maw Maw that I most remember. She always had a dip of "Tube Rose" snuff in her cheek and this yummy, earthy, warm fragrance that was a mixture of liniment for aging knees, wood stove smoke in her hair, and a light rosewater lotion she rubbed on her hands in the morning and at night. She wore hand–laundered, floral-print, cotton dresses that were hosts to sunshine and fresh air from the clothesline. Maw Maw wore dresses every day, even when working at the tobacco barns.

Her impish smile formed creases in her face around bubble cheeks and scrunched her big, dark-brown eyes into little slivers. Her eyes always twinkled as if she knew too many secrets. When I was a toddler, she would fashion a dollhouse from a shoebox and make dolls and clothing out of Kleenex tissue, dotting ink to make eyes and using cardboard and Popsicle sticks to make furniture. She would work for hours on these creations and I would play with them until there was nothing left but tissue shreds. She hummed as she worked and instructed me on how to add furniture as she deftly moved her hands with the stories she spun about the dolly. Her imagination sparked mine. My favorite dolly was a version of me...a 'young girl named Precious, of course, who was born in the country to a farmer and was discovered by a handsome prince who rescued her from pulling tobacco to be his bride and princess —and she always got a couple of new dresses from the Sears catalog.' I remember reading Cinderella and thinking that Maw Maw must have told a lot of people my dolly story since someone took the time to write it all down as a book.

I was her namesake so we had a special bond. You see, my mother won a national essay contest in the seventh grade.

Students who entered the competition were required to use pen names. Maw Maw told her to use Precious and Dare (my mom's middle name) and add "– lyn" to it. Dare-lyn. My mother was so excited when she won the contest that she declared her first daughter would be given this pen name. I used to laugh about how drawn out it could sound when people whined it out at church—Prec-io-us – Da-re-lyn-a. I did not laugh, however, when the girl who sat behind me in third grade said quite loudly, "I don't see anything precious about her-r-r-r."

I loved Sundays, finding a seat in the pew next to Maw Maw in the "big church" service at 11 o'clock. There she would draw a bunny or kitty cat on the back of the church bulletin and hand it to me with the pencil. Occasionally she would curve a mustache on the bunny or kitty and I would laugh out loud. One Sunday we got tickled as we noticed that one of the ladies in the choir had left her large, white earbobs on with her choir robe, apparently a "no-no" in the choir dress code. She didn't notice until the anthem had started and she tried to slip them off while singing the solo part in the song. Maw Maw and I tried to stifle our laughter but we just couldn't, and Paw Paw's face grew red as he tried to separate us. We kept looking around his large frame, eyeballing each other and laughing all the more. He finally got up and left the pew to go get some fresh air. Maw Maw scooted over close to me and we hugged up and paid attention for the rest of the service. I never felt closer to her.

Laughter and music were Maw Maw's signatures. As she aged with Parkinson's disease and her head and hands began to shake uncontrollably, so did her laugh. She always made people feel more comfortable by just acknowledging the trembling in her hands and head. She'd begin rolling her eyes and moving her body as if she were intentionally doing this as a dance and since she was able to make light of it, people relaxed and stopped noticing anything but her sweetness. She was the most real and spiritual person in my life. I never heard her judge anyone. I never heard a cross word from her either. Everyone who knew Maw Maw loved everything about her. She was precious in every way. I am not sure if she was meant to shine her light for everyone she met or just for me, but I loved following her around and chatting away, attracted by the complete force of her love. It was this love and her wisdom I sought when I was young—and, over the years, her wise guidance and reassurance from the spirit world would be there to help me find my way.

Healing Hands

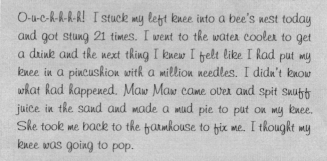

July 16, 1965

Dear Diary,

O-u-c-h-h-h-h! I stuck my left knee into a bee's nest today and got stung 21 times. I went to the water cooler to get a drink and the next thing I knew I felt like I had put my knee in a pincushion with a million needles. I didn't know what had happened. Maw Maw came over and spit snuff juice in the sand and made a mud pie to put on my knee. She took me back to the farmhouse to fix me. I thought my knee was going to pop.

Momma said I got the "bee-hives."

Your friend,

Precious Darelyn Darr

Working with the big, fuzzy, tar-covered leaves was dirty work. Tobacco leaves are like humongous romaine lettuce leaves, only dark green and really heavy. The black tar covering the leaves is almost invisible to the eye, but we knew it was there as it stuck to the hairy arms of the boys who pulled it from the bottom of the six-foot-tall stalks. It coated the women's hands until they were black and gummy to touch. I was a "hander" when I was little, pulling bunches of three equal-sized leaves into a "hand" to be strung on a five-foot–long, broom-handle-looking "tobacco stick." The elders were "stringers," weaving it over and under the stick until it was time to hang it in the barn.

I had almost forgotten that day. I remember Maw Maw healing me with her hands. All the women at the barn started circling around me, batting the swarm of yellow jackets away only to make them buzz and dive all the more. They darted around my head and legs and I was stunned, trying to figure out what was happening—until Maw Maw walked over and calmly spit a long stream of tobacco snuff juice into the sand, waved her handkerchief in the air a few times to shoo the swarm away, and began stirring mud to rub on my knee. She rubbed, spat again, and rubbed some more until my knee was covered with spittle, which dried into a "knee cake."

She took me by the hand and walked me slowly from the tobacco barns through the large cow pasture toward the white plank-board farmhouse, humming all the way. We stopped by the well-house for her to scoop the silver dipper into a bucket of cold water hanging on the spigot. I could feel my left knee swelling beneath the spit balm. She held my small hand which had red streaks. In the kitchen she helped me up onto a wooden stool in front of the big, deep, white sink and spat another brown stream into the palm of her hand. This time she mixed the dark bitter juice with salt and a whole yellow box of baking soda which she kept handy for baking the biscuits I loved. She continued to cover my knee with the gooey stuff as she talked to me about the new kittens born the day before. Her hands were warm as she moved them over my legs and she held them over my bee stings for a long time. I felt my knee heat up and I heard Maw Maw hum something familiar. I felt like I was going to pass out until she put my head on her shoulder and rocked me back and forth while she patted my knee.

Her hands were cooler by the time she was done and she left me sitting alone for a few minutes while she got a cold towel. She wiped the sticky juice off my leg and we counted 21 bee stings. "Lucky number," she said. The hives covering my skin started to fade. "You stay in the house for a little while, Punkin'," she sang, as she patted the top of my head. "Here's some biscuit dough. Why don't you sit at the table and make some little biscuits to bake when we are all done at the barns?"

I felt much better after the biscuits had been pinched into pearls and neatly pressed into place in a small, round, baking pan, so I made my way back to the barn. The women gathered there were gossiping about the lady at the church who was getting fatter and couldn't help it because she was eating to "heal her worries, 'Bless her heart.' " I had learned by now that any lady who received this "blessing" from my aunts was either fat, lazy, being cheated on, cheating on, dumber than mud, or a 'floozie.' I was back into the routine of the workday, and my bee episode faded into the background.

Traveling Dream

July 26, 1965

Dear Diary,

I had a scary dream after sissy, Nikki and I said our prayers. Momma came in for prayers, like always, and she and Daddy were sitting in the living room watching Bonanza and eating banana splits a little later. I could hear them through the thin wall talking and laughing. While I was lying still in bed, right before I was about to go to sleep, my inside angel started jumping up and down on my belly button and then jumped out of my body. I lost my wind and couldn't talk. I could see the top of the house and feel cool air around my face. Then I was high in the sky seeing church steeples and all of Welcome. I flew above the clouds way up into the stars. A silver-and-white rope held me in my body. I thought I was going to die. I hadn't said goodbye to Momma and Daddy, and I knew they would be sad because they loved us more than anything. So, I jumped back into my body and catched my breath.

Your friend,

Precious Darelyn Darr

My inside angel . . . hmmmm, that was an image I had of a miniature version of me, with wings like a fairy, springing up and down on my navel until I just floated out into space, as if I had dived right out of my body into the great cosmic soup, always the starry background for my dreams.

My sister Nikki and I slept in the same bed until I was old enough to leave home. We heard a lot through the walls of our bedroom when Momma and Daddy were sitting on the other side of the wall watching TV or talking about the day.

I remember running into the living room that night, screaming that I thought I was dying and that I hadn't said goodbye to them. It was the second half of Bonanza and Momma and Daddy were raking their bowls as they spooned out the last bites of Breyer's new chocolate ice cream. Momma said "Shhh, honey, you're not dying. Now go back to bed. We're watching Bonanza and you are right here with us so you are not exactly dead. You said your prayers. You are safe, now go back to sleep." I crept back to bed, and held my eyes open, staring at the ceiling until a deep sleep found me.

The next day when I saw Maw Maw and told her about the

dream, she grinned, touched my hand and looked deep into my eyes. "You don't need to be afraid of going to sleep. You are safe in the arms of angels. You will wake up in the morning. Change your bed-time prayer to be your own special prayer. You can add your own words to "Now I lay me down to sleep." While you sleep, your 'inside angel' goes out walking on the wind visiting others, even me. That's a normal thing for you to do, but I wouldn't go telling anybody else that just yet."

Maw Maw said something about "our souls" always being alive. She told me, "You were living before you were even a twinkle in your Momma's and Daddy's eyes." I can't recall if it was then or sometime later that she said all of this, but I vividly remember she believed we have a plan for our lives before we come to Earth, and we are always living, even when our bodies grow old and die. She said sometimes she had a dream where she visited with God and he said that "we are just here to make Him smile." When I asked her, "What do you mean, make Him smile?" she thought for a minute. "God and the angels breathed us on Earth to give witness to the Glory and beauty of His creation. He wanted to share it with us. It says in the story of creation in the Good Book, 'Let Us create the heavens and Earth.' Maybe that 'Us' means us."

Maw Maw got a dreamy, far-away look in her eyes as she spoke more slowly, "I sometimes wonder if it surprised God that He could make a wish, speak some words, and watch the whole world being born. But maybe when He breathed life into Adam and Eve and then we all started being born into bodies, He saw our beauty and smiled." Then she fixed her bright sparkly eyes on me and softly said, "Maybe that's when angels like you decided to come and live here on earth with me and your Momma and Daddy."

Maw Maw's stories always made more sense than all the sermons I heard in church.

Heaven

July 31, 1965

Dear Diary,

I stayed on the farm last night with Maw Maw and Paw Paw. I had the most colorful dream. One minute I was in my room. The next I was in a place I had never been, at least that I can remember.

The place was beautiful. There were big flowers. Not like the snowballs and lilies in Maw Maw's garden—bigger than those. I could smell things in my dream, too. The whole place smelled really nice, like roses and honeysuckle. I wanted to take a breath, a really deep breath, and just hold it forever.

When I woke up, I closed my eyes as tight as I could so I could get back there, but I couldn't.

Your friend,

Precious Darelyn Darr

I didn't have words then to describe what I saw in the dream. I am not sure I do now. It seemed that I was saying my prayers one minute and in an instant I was beamed into an otherworldly place. This place had the most beautiful vistas—lush green landscapes with fields of fragrant flowers—huge flowers, surreal to see against this landscape which felt at once both distant and close. There were streets, including the one that led to a magnificent gate, paved with granulated gem stones, pearlescent in appearance, and these stones drew energy from each step I took – or I was deriving energy from them. They sparkled and rippled under my feet with each step. I stood in front of the gate and looked up. The gate was so tall I could barely see the top which was dotted with large pearls—the size of baseballs—and stones that were breath-taking, capturing light in prisms that sent a rainbow of illumination in every direction.

Maw Maw, Paw Paw and I had a big breakfast that next morning. Breakfast cooked in the farm house was the best smell I could imagine waking up to. Everything Maw Maw cooked tasted a bit like the hickory wood smoke. Scrambled eggs, country ham with red-eye gravy, buttered grits, and biscuits with milk gravy were all effortlessly cooked on the wood stove. Maw Maw and I had churned butter from cow's milk the day before and I remember watching it melt into little streams as it made its way down the mountain of white, stone-ground grits. She poured me a cup of "Granny" coffee—half coffee from the large tin coffee pot on the wood stove, half cream, and two teaspoons of sugar. I poured the coffee into a china saucer so it would cool fast enough to sip. I was trying to remember my dream when she gave me a rare store-bought treat—a Krispy Kreme doughnut to dunk in the coffee for dessert.

When Paw Paw prayed the blessing, which he always did as head of the house, this particular morning he added with a teasing wink, "Biscuits and milk gravy have sent a lot of people to hell." When I looked surprised that he would say something so bold, he added, "Because if it hadn't been for milk gravy and biscuits, they would have died young and innocent." His quips were always followed by a belly laugh, "Tee-Hee-Hee."

When he left for the barns, I told Maw Maw about my dream... well, I started to tell her. She picked up in the middle of my story and touched my hand like she always did before she said something important. She looked into my eyes in a way that made me feel like she saw me from the inside out. She finished telling me exactly what I had seen – every detail, just as if she had been there in the dream with me. I had goose bumps.

She had been there on the path. It was Maw Maw who I had felt guiding me in my dream. "I believe this is heaven," she said, "and I have seen it many times. When your uncle was in the navy, I knew he was in trouble one time. I could just feel it. I saw him swimming in the sea. His ship had been hit by a torpedo. I had this dream that night and I woke up feeling everything would be all right. I could see his face from inside this place and while I knew he was in danger, I also knew he was going to come home. I think this place is our true home—heaven—the home for our souls."

Ouija

Dear Diary,   August 5, 1965

Cousin Kathy and I had a pajama party last night and played with the Ouija Board.

I asked it if I will marry Grant. He is my boyfriend. We played spin the bottle at my other cousin's birthday party and he was there. The bottle stopped pointed toward me and he kissed me on the mouth.

The Ouija said "No" real fast.

It also said I would have 2 babies. I love kids, so I hope I will have more than 2. Cousin Kathy said she wasn't going to have any kids but the Board said "2" for her too.

I wonder who I'll marry? I hope he is a movie star.
Your friend,

Precious Darelyn Darr

Grant became a "Hell's Angel" when he dropped out of high school. Good call Ouija Board!

Just A Game

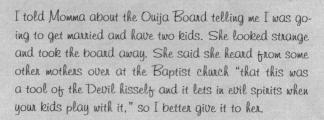

August 6, 1965

Dear Diary,

I told Momma about the Ouija Board telling me I was going to get married and have two kids. She looked strange
and took the board away. She said she heard from some
other mothers over at the Baptist church "that this was
a tool of the Devil hisself and it lets in evil spirits when
your kids play with it," so I better give it to her.

I thought it was just a game. Momma and Daddy were fine
with me playing with it since Christmas, but something must
have changed.

It does feel like it has a mind of its own. It's good we
got rid of it before the Devil hisself got to us. There are
times I worry that I might just go flying out of my body...

and I definitely don't want to live with the Devil.

I also want to tell you something terrible, Diary.

I feel like I am adopted. I looked for my birth certificate
last week, and Momma caught me searching her bottom
dresser drawer. She showed me the certificate and said
I "was born to her and Daddy and quit trying to escape."
We both laughed when she said it.

I just feel so odd sometimes, like I don't belong here.

Your friend,

Precious Darelyn Darr

I believe I came to my parents as part of my life journey and contract, but there were times when I was growing up that I didn't feel
like I belonged anywhere. Looking back now, even though I have
often felt like an outsider, there was no place more grounding than
my home. I loved the time I spent with my folks even after I was
grown, yet sometimes when I'd visit Welcome, I felt like I was having an out-of-body experience. It was home, yet it was also
a community stuck in the 50's. Women's hair was teased into upright
and locked positions, perfectly sprayed into styles once a week at
the local beauty shops. I remember they used so much hair spray
at the beauty shops that a fog followed my mom home after she
got her hair coiffed on Fridays for the weekend's church services.

People punched toothpicks in their teeth when they left the
local Bar-B-Que joints, letting them dangle like cigarettes as they
chatted about the meal, or gossiped about their kinfolk on the way
to their cars—and the fine people of Welcome loved their cars.

□ ◇ □ ◇ □ ◇ □ ◇ □ ◇ □ ◇ □ ◇ □ ◇ □ ◇ □ ◇ □ ◇ □ ◇ □ ◇ □ ◇ □ ◇ □ ◇ □ ◇ □ ◇ □

Seeing Things

September 12, 1972

Dear Diary,

A car! I got my first car today! She's a white (and rusted out) 1962 Chevy II. Daddy bought her from my geometry teacher, Mrs. Payne, for $150. He's going to overhaul the engine and put recapped tires on her this week. I am going to have her painted and get the seats upholstered. I'll have to clean more houses and teach baton lessons to more elementary majorettes this year, but I've saved almost $250 and that should be a start. I also get paid $15 for each newspaper column I write for the Lexington Dispatch and that's once a week, so it will add up. I'm calling her "Ole Bessie." Daddy helped me name her. Maw Maw said every car should have a name. When we name our cars, they seem to take on a personality...and she says giving your car a name protects the driver.

Everyone must love their first set of wheels. I felt lucky just to have the freedom to come and go as I pleased. Cars were a serious investment in Welcome. Most of the guys I knew, had saved a couple of summer's worth of pay from two jobs to get their first one and the school parking lot was covered with Cougars, TransAms, and Mustangs.

The first few weeks I had "Ole Bessie" I got caught behind our school bus on the way up Hwy 52. The shift lever was on the steering column and I couldn't change gears smoothly or get the hang of pressing the clutch in rhythm with moving the gear stick so I ground gears a lot. Bessie would jump from first gear into third all the way to school. Kids gathered in the back of the buses in front of me to point and laugh. It was so embarrassing that my sister and friends preferred to take the bus and laugh with the others instead of riding with me.

The first memory I have of driving Bessie further than the two miles to school was driving to our planning meeting for the junior class homecoming float. The stars were especially bright out in the country and that night one star was really big and luminous. It appeared to be dancing with me as I drove the back roads through the country. It came so close that I felt I could reach out and touch it. Then it started moving fast, zig-zagging in and out of trees. It got larger, and I realized it wasn't a star. I rolled down the window to see if I could hear a sound. Nothing. I rolled the window up and started talking to Bessie, "Just let me get there safe and sound. Take good care of me, Ole Bessie," I prayed.

Goose bumps covered my body and my brain raced. I thought to myself, "Do I turn around and go back home or stay on the road to Debbie's house in Arcadia?" I was so close to being there. I drove with one eye shut, as fast as I could without losing control. When I got to the house, the light appeared to be shaped like a disc.

It stopped behind the trees. I bolted into the house with hair standing up on the back of my neck wondering if 'My Favorite Martian' was about to jump out of the bushes. I poked my head outside. Nothing. I must have been seeing things.

I wanted to tell everyone what had just happened but when I opened my mouth, nothing came out. A few friends laughed about a joke someone told and we kept working on the plans for the Homecoming Parade. As I looked around the room, everyone was acting normal—as normal as high school juniors can be—gossiping, planning, and laughing at each other's stories. My neighbor Mike followed me home after the meeting. Nothing unusual. My mind rationalized the event. I wished Bessie could talk. I looked at her grill and headlights, and she seemed to smile. I thanked her for keeping me safe. It took a while for me to get ready for bed. I sat in the bathtub and soaked until the water got cold. I peeked out the small bathroom window at the moonlit backyard. Everything looked bright and safe, so I went to bed. But at some level I think I knew that this was a sign that we were not alone and that there was something much more to this life than what I had been taught so far. But where were the people who would talk openly about seeing spaceships? They certainly weren't in Welcome.

Even though I felt like it was real, there was no place to tell this story so that people wouldn't call me a total airhead.

Hot Dogs

November 11, 1972

Dear Diary,

No more sightings. Maybe I WAS just seeing things. I hear the government has some new satellite weather thingies they keep sending up into space as part of our NASA's programs. It was probably one of those.

Ole Bessie got a new coat of paint and looks really sharp. Sandi and I drove her to Speedy's Bar-B-Que Drive-In after the basketball game tonight.

We parked next to some seniors from other high schools. We rolled down the window as we put on our pale, pink lipstick in the hopes of catching a glimpse of the cute new guy who just moved here from Atlanta. He stepped out of the back door to the kitchen and came right over to Bessie, with a pencil behind his ear, a white paper boat hat topping his curly brown hair, and a dirty apron draped around his Levis. He put the tray on the window and started, "Ladies, you here for slaw dogs?" "Uh-huh," I heard Sandi say all dreamy.

I drooled, "I'll take mine all the way. Mustard, chili, slaw, and onions, with extra-done fries and a Cheerwine please."

"Yes Ma'am, Ladies," he said as he jogged back to the kitchen to put in the order.

The hot dogs were out a few minutes later, wrapped in kitchen paper so all the fixins were smashed inside the bun. I don't know if it's the smell of hickory wood smoke, or the dogs, but I felt like I was in heaven. I just wanted to watch "cute boy" work the parking lot. We chewed really slow and groaned like we were at an old, Elvis movie.

"I'll be back to check on you in a few," the cute one winked as he left, half jogging back to the kitchen, his jeans hugging every perfect muscle.

"I just want to wrap my long arms around him," I heard from the seat next to me, but I dared not take my eyes off his perfect backside.

"I just want to take a picture of his backside...or maybe even kiss him."

We both laughed. We don't even know his name.

Sandi said, dreamy-like, "Sometimes you just got to get a Dog!"

Your friend,

Precious Danelyn Darr

P.S. Diary, I hope no one finds you!

I travel back home for the food because there is more love in a meal there than anyplace on earth. And sometimes I still make my way to Speedy's for a hot dog. The cute boys are now older members of AARP but they still bounce in and out of the swinging kitchen door. You still get a tray hung on your window with sandwiches and well-done fries and it still takes just a beep of your horn to have the tray taken away. The hot dogs arrive wrapped in white kitchen paper and, of course, as always in my memory, they just simply melt in your mouth like a fine delicacy. Occasionally I travel back there and remember the simplicity of being in touch with every one of my senses.

Catching Up

There were times in my life when I wrote in my diary all the time, and there were years when I wrote nothing. When I picked up my journal after a long dry spell, I sometimes felt obligated to catch up —so I could start writing again. This entry was one of those. It leaves out a lot of the events of my life, and maybe one day the novel will be written that captures all those stories—a marriage to a high school pal, a musical we wrote together, a divorce, and my finding my way away from all that had been familiar—things that were life changing and worth writing about. In fact, many of those events were chapters in the 1,400-page "War and Peace" version I had written over the course of a few years. But for now...this entry captured my need to reset the stage for parking my thoughts again in my trusted journal.

September 1982

Hello Old Friend & Diary,

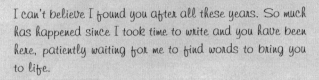

I can't believe I found you after all these years. So much has happened since I took time to write and you have been here, patiently waiting for me to find words to bring you to life.

We live in Raleigh now, you and me...just the two of us. We have a duplex apartment behind Crabtree Mall. I moved here to take a new job as the Sales Manager for the Satellite Division of a broadcast company. Here's the CliffsNotes version of what's happened since I wrote:

• Auditioned for and won two scholarships to study drama at local universities — wasn't able to take either, needed to go to work first

• Married high school friend and sweetheart — it was the "next thing to do" - -everybody else was

• Became youth director and secretary of 1st Baptist Church

• Wrote church-type musical called, "As John Saw It," with young husband

• Divorced husband four years later - - whole community in uproar, momma tried to save me from myself and help me save face with the church

- Worked at Belks, then at the mall, then at the Rainy Day Boutique in Hyatt House in Winston-Salem

- Went to community college and took other classes at night

- Went to work as a sales rep for WXYZ-FM radio — promoted to Sales Manager within 4 months

- Company sold to Nationwide Insurance (I was the only female manager in radio and TV). Couldn't understand my new boss after first two weeks. Horrible temper. He pulled me over my desk by my collar when he got angry at me for questioning him about political rates. Long story. Moved to Raleigh to work in Capitol Broad casting — cool boss, good company. Christened the satellite "Uplink" last year (with a Pepsi bottle—the owner doesn't drink alcohol) — so Pepsi, "the taste born in the Carolinas," splattered everywhere. Love the owner and my new boss.

- Met Italian boyfriend, Vito at my old radio station job (see him now only on weekends — It's okay because I travel a lot with the new job.)

- Took my first flight ever to New York City four years ago and have been traveling ever since

- Lots of time alone, so maybe I will write more now. Thanks for waiting for me, Diary. Glad I found you again!

We apparently live three or four lifetimes before we are 30 years old, trying to find our way, sorting out our internal characters and roles until we find those that best fit. Mine included being a playwright / actor / performer, a wife and daughter-in-law, a display artist for a department store chain, a Sunday School Teacher/Youth Leader, and a sales person. So much happened to me in such a short period of time. Two universities offered me scholarships to study theatre after my high school Drama and English teachers took me to audition. If I ever had a "broken dream," it was that I never pursued that path, settling instead for a proposal of marriage from my high school pal the night of my senior prom and then a job right out of high school. I planned a big southern wedding with my pal and a wedding party of 18 others. He was a scholarship-winning college freshman and my friends, even those who were betrothed or married around the same time, left for college to earn teaching degrees. The agreement with my husband was that I would work while he went to school and then he would work to put me through school after he graduated. We were married four days before my 20th birthday and moved into a small mobile home on his grandfather's farm. I went to work in retail, paying the bills, tithing to the church and occasionally bouncing checks at the local grocery store because we couldn't make ends meet.

By the time my studious husband was preparing to graduate college I had ended up in a designer boutique, thanks to someone noticing my work at the department store and arranging for an interview with the owners. Late one afternoon after I had worked at the boutique for a few months, a dapper-dressed gentleman escorting two beautiful thirty-year-old petite women walked in and told me to fix them up with whatever they wanted. He left to shop in the adjacent men's store and I worked past closing time suiting the ladies up with Diane von Furstenberg dresses, Nipon suits, and a couple of evening gowns. They were both "giddy" happy. My hunch was that their giddiness was due to the bottle of wine they had shared before they started shopping and the fact that they looked amazing in anything they tried on in their perfect size-four bodies. I wrapped packages totaling over $8,000 and gave the bill to their escort. He smiled and pulled enough cash from his wallet to cover it. Then he told me that he liked the way I worked, "the way I handled myself," and asked if I would I be interested in "working for him."

So there I was standing behind a cash register with half my annual salary in my hand and with no idea what he was really offering—what I would need to do, or un-do—to "work" for him. He saw my concern and quickly offered, "I own radio stations. These two amazing women have just won a monthly sales contest and I am paying up."

Mr. "Boss" now had my attention. Three weeks after the most unusual interview of my life, I began working for his FM station. He interviewed me in his garden apartment home furnished with white sofas and bookshelves that surrounded the place holding vintage books lined up in categories. A spiral staircase led from his apartment to the one below, where one of the women who had earned the shopping spree lived. As it turned out, she was the station manager and a "very good friend" of Mr. Boss. After the interview, he suggested that we go take a look at my new place of employment. When we arrived at the renovated service station that had been turned into radio studios, there was a burning cross on the lawn of the AM gospel and news station he had just sold to a former employee, an African-American female. "Those crazy kids, you never know what pranks they will play next," he said off-handedly, as we drove around to the back of the stations and parked.

The gravel parking lot backed up to an outdoor, XXX-rated, drive-in movie theater. There is likely nothing more mortifying and disorienting than the combination of a perverted sex scene and a burning cross to influence my first impressions of this strange world I could be stepping into. The images that flashed across the XXX screen stayed with me as I followed Mr. Boss into the basement of the two-story concrete building that housed two radio studios. AM upstairs with offices, FM downstairs with one executive office and a large room with desks lining the perimeter. Finding words to express what I was experiencing was difficult, but I tried to keep a sense of good humor. He went upstairs to call the authorities about the cross burning on the lawn and I looked around the stark concrete-block basement serving as the sales office. There were no windows. It felt like a trap. I wanted to be anywhere but there. I was terrified. Then I saw Kitty, the stunning, jazz show host I had listened to since she made her debut a year earlier and she warmly welcomed me to come sit with her. Being inside a radio studio and watching the show unfold was contagious. It was theatre, and I wanted to be a part of it. I took the sales job the next day when things were quite normal at the studio—no movies playing in the background, no crosses burning on the lawn. Normal. I met people from all over the country who worked to make this a thriving enterprise; they explained their jobs to me, and I was hooked.

The next few years whirled by as I learned a new business and diverted my attention from the cinematic sex scenes that met me as I left the office after dark most nights. I also got over the curiosity of trying to determine which air personality was steaming up the windows of the large Buick with flat tires which had found a permanent home in the gravel parking lot.

During this period of time, something happened to me that I suppose happens to us all at some point. There was an energy shift—a basic change in me. I started listening to my heart instead of to what others thought I "should do." I left my high school pal and young husband behind after realizing that we had just somewhat mechanically "taken the next step" when we married, and that I was not likely to move too far away from our mobile home or have too many other adventures in life if I stayed put. I also gave up being a youth director for the church. It felt wrong that I was divorced and still tried to hold that position. That was something "we" did together. Although I was scared, I felt liberated and excited and I was making a nice sum of money that gave me possibilities I had never dreamed of.

So I moved in with a new friend and colleague, one of the lovely gals who had shopped in the boutique—just until I found my own place. And I bought a Saab sports car. Of course it wasn't all peaches and cream. I saw a therapist to deal with the pending divorce and the fact that I was receiving letters from Momma, complete with Bible quotes that were written when she couldn't sleep at night for worrying about me. She and Daddy were struggling, trying to figure out how to help me patch things up and get my life back together and be "a good Christian." I felt her heart breaking and it broke mine, but I had to keep following my intuition. I couldn't live any other way. I really didn't have a clue how all of this would turn out, yet I was committed to something I couldn't see, or explain. I had to keep moving in this direction. Something inside me was guiding me as if I had no other choice. I went to another church, but didn't go to the front for the altar call. I didn't feel wrong or sinful, just sad about the broken relationships and yet hopeful that something else great was awaiting me.

The radio station had a growth spurt and I became the Sales Manager after just four months in my new position. I wrapped myself in this new world and in my work. Two years later the business was worth a lot of money and it was sold to a national insurance company that could afford to pay cash for the property. This may have been great for the owner, but I was sad again. I had just found my place, and now my future was in the hands of some broadcasting guys from Ohio who seemed at best to be amused by my southern lilt and stilettos.

The personal journey I had begun had personal costs and they were being revealed. I still loved to visit Maw Maw even though she was in declining health. After suffering two strokes and a heart attack she was unable to speak, so when I visited her I did all of the talking. I sang. I held her hand. She always blinked in gratitude. Occasionally, a tear would find its way down the creases around her still-sparkly brown eyes.

Maw Maw Leaves

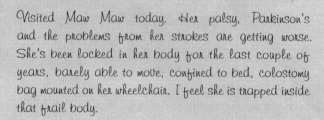

Christmas 1982

Dear Diary,

Visited Maw Maw today. Her palsy, Parkinson's and the problems from her strokes are getting worse. She's been locked in her body for the last couple of years, barely able to move, confined to bed, colostomy bag mounted on her wheelchair. I feel she is trapped inside that frail body.

I still see the light in her eyes, though, even though the last stroke left her without speech.

She grabbed my hand today and just held tight for a long time.

I hate that she suffers, but maybe she visits our "heaven" place more often now. She once told me that "all is well there." No suffering, no pain, no fear.... only love.

I sang our favorite song, "Froggie Went A Courtin'" softly in her ear before leaving. She smiled. My new boyfriend Vito said on the way home that she had so much love in her eyes, he could feel our bond. (I haven't told you about him, Diary. I met him at the radio station. He is so handsome!)

It's really sad to see Maw Maw go deeper into this state. She has the sweetest spirit. She seems grateful to be alive, even while trapped in a strange, twisted body.

Maw Maw died April 30th, 1983. Her funeral was held at Beulah United Church of Christ two days later. As I looked at her body laid out in the casket, I didn't feel sad. Instead, I felt she had been liberated. I was almost joyful. The service was sweet but I didn't feel the new minister knew her very well. The songs sounded empty. The stories were missing her essence, her humor.

During the service I smelled her rosewater lotion and her Tube Rose snuff. I felt she was hovering around me, so I got a pencil and drew a kitty cat with a mustache on the back of the funeral service bulletin. I felt her spirit swirl around me, and I swear I could hear her giggle. Tears welled up and stung the back of my nose and eyes. As we made our way to the grave site behind the church, I saw a pair of doves hover over the white funeral tent. How Precious, I thought to myself. They cooed and stayed around until the service was over. I didn't hear a word the preacher said.

Paw Paw cried a lot and quoted scripture when we got back to the farmhouse. The whole day felt strange to me. I closed my eyes and tried to see her when she was healthy, sitting on the bedside in the front room of the farm house, playing the guitar—making up songs and verses just for me.

BOOK II
LEAPS

My view now about
Leaps of Faîth

He looked at me. Never mind there were 25,000 others in the arena. Bruce looked at me and from somewhere below his deep brown eyes, his yummy soulful music filled me as he gazed into my eyes, singing to me as if we were the only two people in the arena in Chapel Hill.

Listening to this 1992 concert sealed for me something that I had reckoned with much of my young adult life. I had talked about faith, but there were times when I was challenged to exhibit it, not the show up at church faith, but the total trust that I would be OK, if I would simply take a "leap" once in a while.

Oh, I know this Springsteen song was about seduction, but it also resonated with me about some of the decisions I'd made over the past decade. Bruce was the story teller of my life in so many ways. Looking back now, I realize that taking a leap of faith for me meant I had to learn to trust others, but more importantly —myself —totally, without excuse or explanation. I needed to show some guts in the choices I made in even the simplest, day-to-day challenges of living a lie or living the truth, and I had to move in the direction of what called to me, even when it didn't make a lot of sense or fit my traditional values. I learned to move quickly in the direction of what felt warm and right, and away from cold and hard.

And over time, I took more leaps.

From this present view that has served me.

Here, Read This

July 30th, 1983

Dear Diary,

Today I flew home from Chicago and a strange thing happened in O'Hare Airport on my way to the departure gate. I had stopped in a newsstand to buy some gum. A very tall, blonde, blue-eyed woman who looked about 6'-8" or so, dressed to the nines in a light grey suit, (with no handbag or briefcase) walked up to me, handed me a paperback book and said, "Here, read this. It was meant for you."

I glanced down at the book, <u>Out on a Limb</u> by Shirley MacLaine and then looked up to inquire why she thought so, but she was gone. I looked around the newsstand and peered down the concourse both ways. No sign of her. She had simply vanished.

Apparently, this was worth the twelve bucks, if just for the curiosity. I paid for my gum and the book. As I buckled my seat belt on the plane and opened the book to begin reading, I smelled Rosewater lotion and Tube Rose snuff.

I told the guy in the seat next to me about how the book was recommended and about the woman disappearing. He smiled nervously and asked me if I "still believe in Santa Claus, too?" and closed his eyes to make me disappear.

From now on, I'll keep these stories between you and me, Diary.

That book, like others since, awakened me to a more conscious way of seeing the world. I read the entire book in less than a day. I had goose bumps much of the time I read it. No other book had spoken to me in such a profound way. The experiences MacLaine wrote about were familiar to me:

> "I continually encountered a deep need for spirituality and expanded consciousness, a need for people to come together, to share their energies in something that worked. I found people had had experiences similar to mine; people involved with trance channeling, past life recall, growing spiritual awareness and even contact with UFOs. I found spiritual communities were springing up all over the world . . ." [2]

The details of her journey and her inquiry indicated that she had researched texts written about ancient civilizations and spiritual quests. She shared this very personal and intimate journey without understanding at the time the impact it would have on people like me or the tremors this exposure would have on her life and her career. I read the book again, parts of it aloud to my Italian Catholic, "Vito," who humored me and engaged in conversations about the content. I couldn't tell if this was his idea of a good time, but he was patient with me as I explored every book I could find on the concepts raised by MacLaine. He read most of them as well and we had lively conversations about the truths and the myths, and the bridges these new thoughts offered to lingering questions from our childhood traditions. Some of the constraints of my religious upbringing fell away. Many of the questions I had as a child were being answered in my reading and research. Bible passages almost seemed to be illuminated when I read them, particularly ones that dealt with "being born again." This phrase was translated in new ways – being born again into the world of spirit, being born again in our perspectives, or perhaps being literally born again into the world of humans to experience a new life with new circumstances and lessons. These were all possibilities I had not really considered before—except when Maw Maw looked at me with that light in her eyes, from the inside out and interpreted my dreams.

Everything was possible from this view. Maybe we are a part of a Divine Design—a project, a study in consciousness, an evolution of the spirit, with the ability for our spirits to come back into other bodies in the way actors bring to life many characters for movies, yet are still the same person. My life became a continuous prayer and I opened myself to guidance from a universal source and from others who had always been present, or who were showing up as guides, such as the grey-suited woman in the airport.

I welcomed miracles. I started smiling at the coincidences and daily occurrences that I now recognized as being spirit-inspired. In one moment of inspiration I scratched this note in my diary:

God is everywhere and in everything. There is no place God is not—and in everything that is happening to me, around me, within me, God is present. And maybe, like Maw Maw said, "we are just here to entertain God, to make Him smile."

"God is everywhere and in everything." I wonder if this is true, or if there are two tracks of creation: the Universe, flowing along with all the resources we need to access for all time. And then a powerful being who operates somewhat like we do... thinking, smiling, and waving His big ole hand in the air with some kind of magic wand?

The engineer of the radio station explained to me once, as a part of my training, how radio waves work and how radio signals travel. "Yup," he said, "they go everywhere. If you have enough metal in your mouth you might be able to tune in your favorite station just by standing still in the right place long enough." Ka-ching. I pulled out the site map for our tower and studied the radio waves the engineer had hand drawn on the map. I thought about how the waves run through buildings and over land—how they travel over and through every inch of space around us. One of those insights flashed before me as a thought: "We are pure energy forms, unconsciously and constantly emitting our own vibes and receiving all sorts of signals all of the time. We are both transmitters and receivers, sending and receiving energy in the form of thoughts and intentions, creating realities unconsciously in our mindless conversations. We are divining our futures, creating relationships by the messages we send and those thoughts we allow to find homes in our minds and bodies, sent out on those waves. Each annunciation or declaration, each prayer sent on the wings of angels into the grand cosmic soup is an invitation and a creation. Each thought of hatred we harbor attracts similar energetic reactions. This is simply the cause-and-effect relationship we study in science and that we apply to just about everything, except how we function as spiritual beings." This is why people can literally pick up on each other's vibes or vibrations—this is how we connect energetically.

I recall this notion hit me at the time like a huge "ah-ha!," and it came from both within me and from somewhere way beyond me—as if the message had been absorbed into my being for later translation, perhaps in this story. It just happened to be a bigger idea than any I remember considering before that day.

Angels in the City

August 10th, 1983

Dear Diary,

I just got home from New York City. My sister Nikki and my best friend Dana were with me for a girls' weekend. It was the first time Nikki had ever flown and her first trip to New York.

We saw 42nd Street, the Broadway musical, and as we exited the theatre we turned left at Times Square, walking and talking, not paying too much attention. I was uneasy after a few blocks as some shady-looking people started pressing around us. I asked the girls if they thought we had made a wrong turn. I told them I thought our hotel was in the other direction.

"No, no - it's this way," Dana said.

I noticed red and pink lights on the porches of the old brownstone apartments opening to the street. I said a mental prayer for protection. An instant later, two of New York's finest police officers rounded the corner and walked up to us. Without an ounce of hesitation, one looked straight into my eyes and asked, "You ladies take a wrong turn?"

I felt relief as I looked into the bluest eyes I have ever seen. "Yes, officer, I think we did." The other one turned to call a taxi and within a nano-second, a Yellow Cab pulled to the curb. As I looked up to thank them, I noticed for the first time that they were twins—seven-foot-tall, identical twins. Dana and Nikki kept chatting. I felt like I had one foot in this world and one in another. I told the cab driver we wanted to go to the Sheraton at Times Square. He smiled and hit the meter. Next to the meter, I saw his nametag, which read Mikael. No last name. There was a small, pewter Jesus statue on the dashboard. I turned again to wave at the officers. They were gone, just like their sister at the Chicago airport. A hint of Tube Rose snuff wafted through the taxi as the driver pulled away from the curb.

Is this a game? A big cosmic game we are playing with angels dropping in now and then to keep us on course?

This was probably the first time I thought we might be playing a game—an exquisite game that we help design as we go along. I get scared and say a prayer and two very tall twins and a cab show up to help me along my way. I intend something from my heart, on a whim, and whatever that is... shows up. I think of someone and they call me, out of the blue.

What I have intended, what I've prayed for, believing it is possible and within my reach, has shown up. I just have to stop, notice, and appreciate the miracle of it. What I have found is that when I move in the direction of what feels like the right thing to do, when I pay attention to that still small voice, then a bigger step or opportunity—or miracle—than those I might imagine presents itself to me. And on occasion, that miracle has given me an experience that opens a bigger door.

Seeing Things Again

June 4th, 1984

Dear Diary,

Where to begin? I received an invitation a few weeks ago to a seminar on Extraterrestrials at Wake Forest University. Vito was also invited, as was my friend Paula. When we arrived we followed yellow signs to an auditorium-style classroom in a new building on campus. I recognized a few other people, but for the most part, the 50 or so people were all new faces.

Marc B, the seminar leader, was a slight, very fair-skinned young man who told his personal story of growing up in upstate New York. His story began with his description of his home and a backyard that connected to the school playground behind his house. He told of how he woke up frequently as a child with a small ball of golden light dancing in his room. It seemed harmless, and it was also playful, so he became curious. After this went on for awhile, the light started getting bigger and seemed to beckon him to follow it. He and his dog would traipse behind it to the playground. After doing so a number of times, he started receiving thoughts that this dancing light was connected with a spaceship. He felt that this was a probe, sent ahead of the ship to connect with Marc as a messenger. Marc began to communicate through telepathy—sending mental questions and receiving answers about "why they were here."

As I listened to Marc weave his story, I began to notice several things occurring in the room. First, I saw a white beam of light shoot from his hands every time he touched a whiteboard or moved his arms in expression. Then I saw a large white aura around his body. I could smell sweat, as if no one in the room was wearing deodorant. No, it wasn't sweat, but a pungent odor as if the human costume had decayed and given birth to the scent of a musky candle. And then I saw others appearing in the room. Some were standing, and some were sitting behind us on the steps that ran between the seats. He stopped his story and acknowledged that there were others among us — others who some of us would see and have an experience of, and that some would not. He also said that among us were members of a government agency who traveled with him or showed up whenever he spoke to invited groups- this was part of the reason we were not all introduced. I looked at Vito who seemed interested, but was clearly not having the same experience I was. If he was anything other than mildly curious, it was not apparent by the expression on his face.

Marc illustrated for us the journey he had taken to communicate with ETs. His persistent question as a child was specifically, "Why are you here?" The answers that came to him were simply, "We are here to help humans wake up and to help heal the Earth. The damage to the ozone is very real and if Earth is damaged, there will be a ripple effect throughout this solar system and the larger universe. There was another planet in this solar system called Maldec that was annihilated by its inhabitants long ago. The moons that have been brought into this solar system were brought by others like us to remedy the imbalance created by this explosion, this cosmic void. These moons are hollow and are not made of the same elements as the planets in the solar system, including Earth. Your astronauts and scientists now know and can confirm this."

Marc said that as he grew to understand and trust these conversations with "others" he began seeing spaceships, and the light he would see from airplanes would bend as he photographed it through his airplane window. He was instructed telepathically to do these things. He showed some photographs taken from airline windows, in which the light against the background of starlit nights was bent in the form of big Zs.

Vito thought aloud that these might be enhanced photographs. I sat and stared with goose bumps running the length of my arms.

Much of the rest of this day and the stories about "others" rang from true to absurd to me and to my friends. Most of it, however, felt real and urgent. And I allowed in my mind that everything he said was possible when I realized the musky odor was stronger and I smelled like I had been working in the tobacco fields in the heat of the day. The room was cool and I had been sitting, as had others, but the distracting body odor was also mine and the "others" inside the room were disappearing, evaporating.

When the session ended, we all piled into cars and headed out to Hanging Rock, where we planned to have a potluck dinner, and where Marc intended to "call space-ships". Our car load stopped at a service station for me to deodorize and to pick up some food for the potluck. Fortunately, Charles Chips, Krispy Kreme doughnuts, and Sweet Tea were available inside, so that was our contribution. We arrived at Hanging Rock State Park, just outside of Winston-Salem, at dusk to find that the other attendees had actually cooked, and we supped on fine vegetarian tofu and spinach dishes. It was a really cloudy night, and it felt a bit chilly for June. Marc and a host of the attendees had been there the night before to check out the location and they indicated there was a tremendous show of lights and ships waiting for us, based on what they'd seen. I anticipated something magical, since they had obviously seen some cool stuff and came back to talk about it.

Marc sat out on a large, rocky ledge, where we gathered. He turned a flashlight on and shined it into space, which he explained made him feel he was doing something to 'call them' but that he had been told wasn't needed. I had a small audio recorder with me and turned it on to see if I could capture something, anything that would give me evidence to share.

Nothing

Nothing

Nothing

Then thick clouds rolled in and out over us.

I searched the sky, waiting, wanting to see something more. A crunch of leaves and twigs in the nearby woods caught my attention. Paula had decided to take a walk earlier and as I turned to see her coming toward me, something else caught my attention. Maw Maw was walking behind her in a floral print dress, her hair wrapped into the hair hat, white light shining around her. I wanted to run to her, but she disappeared over the ledge before I could make the connection. Goose-bump-type energy ran through my arms and legs, up my spine and into the base of my skull. "Maw Maw," I whispered, but she never reappeared.

Fifteen more minutes of waiting, eyes fixed on the thick clouds. More nothing, just quiet mumblings and people shifting their weight on the rocks.

Then it appeared. A neon spider-like thing—glowing blue, green and white light, with tentacles moving in and out, up and around. There was no whirling noise, just the sound of a thick silence. It was there for 90 seconds, perhaps two minutes. Then it was gone. When I checked my recorder later, the only sound was a collective gasp for air from those of us who witnessed it.

I still get goose bumps when I remember this event.

Marc B. told us that this was a probe, sent from a mother ship. He said that often these are sent ahead so that those who see can believe and be prepared to see more, and so that those who are not ready to see will be able to explain it away, which is exactly what happened.

Among those of us who saw the probe, there were varying descriptions. Many more saw nothing. When I saw the movie <u>Men in Black</u> many years after this experience, I laughed harder than most when I saw the flashing thing, the "neutralizer" that erases the ET experience so people could get on with their "normal" routines. Maybe that's what happens – we see it and then we can't recall it because in some way the memory of it is erased or maybe the experience of it has no place to land in our brains. In other words, perhaps we are mentally incapable of shaping and articulating such events in our current language. I wondered about those natives who first saw sea-going ships from the explorers. What did they think? How did they explain the visit? Were they frightened? How did they accept those aliens who became "us?"

And Maw Maw—what was the symbolism of her visit? I'm not sure that I will ever understand this, other than to trust that anytime I've gone out on a ledge, or a limb, or taken a wrong turn, she has been there to guide me back to where I need to be...to bring me home. Most of the time she has been an essence, a smell of tobacco and lotion. This time she had been more. Perhaps she was assuring me, giving me a sense of peace.

During the following week, I told a few people about the experience as best as I could. They wanted to believe me, but it was apparent that most didn't or couldn't. Over time I just stopped telling the story. However, it gave me hope to know that out there somewhere are "others" who are interested in helping us wake up, so that we don't upset the natural order of an expanding universe and of this beautiful planet we call home. I wondered then as now, when they will make themselves known, other than in the images on our movie screens or in science fiction illustrations.

Men

October 18th, 1984

Dear Diary,

Guilt . . . Guilt . . . Guilt . . . I am feeling very confused and really yucky. "I will do better to stay faithful, loyal, and true." I will write that 200 times.

I'm planning a wedding, for crying out loud! We have set the date for Memorial Day next year. Less than 8 months from now "Vito" and I will be exchanging nuptials. But something must be missing, right?

I have been seeing Charles, a charming, local ad exec, purely as a friend, until it got complicated last night. He is yummy—dark and swarthy. We've been to the Governor's ball, several large ad events, the premier of the movie Brainstorm...and he is a fabulous escort, a total gentleman. Vito was okay with me going, since we still have the long-distance thing. But oh my, Charles kissed me last night and I melted into my shoes. We were totally platonic until then. Now, I am conflicted.

I am scaring myself. I really care about Charles. We laugh a lot. I told my friend Marilyn about my predicament, and she said to marry the one that "makes you laugh." I laugh with both of them! So now I am looking at the two of them, and feel I love them both. How can that happen if I am committed? I am committed! I will write that 200 times. HELP!

I called my friend Marilyn, who was the best resource in my life. She was connected to everyone, from hairdressers (although I will never forgive her for the one that fried my hair with bleach under a dryer and then cut it into a very short spiky "do" to cover the sins) to therapists. She suggested a therapist. Seeing a professional helped me understand transactional analysis—how different relationships draw out various dimensions of who we are. Charles was the person in my life attracted to my inner child. Vito was the parent—chivalrous, protective, taking care of me as if he had placed me in a gilded cage. She said that what was missing was the person who could just be an adult and treat me like an adult. I needed to work on having that aspect in my relationships with these wonderful men. And she agreed to work with Vito and me to make sure we were on the right path.

□ ◇ ■

The One

February 14th, 1985

Dear Diary,

I am still sorting out the duplicitous relationships. I have worked with a therapist and committed myself to Vito, and I've stopped seeing Charles. I have gone to work for Charles' dad at radio station WXYZ-FM, so it's probably for the best, although I am around him more now than before, so it is hard to stay focused sometimes. Marriage is just the next step for me. I will be 30 in June. It is time, right?

I saw a "counseling intuitive" yesterday with my old room-mate Paula, who was in town on business. The intuitive was a very sweet Japanese woman. When I posed my questions about "how I could love two people at the same time," and "if I was on the right track with Vito," she checked into my energy, said a quiet prayer, and looked into my eyes for a few minutes before saying anything else. Then she perked up, and the first phrase out of her mouth was, "Oh, so many nice men, so little time." When she smiled, she appeared to be missing some of her teeth.

I listened to her, even though I was somewhat skeptical, because I wanted to understand my heart. She gave me insights on both men. Vito was a karmic relationship. She said he was my soul mate in many ways, but he could have a tendency to smother me—or, to say it another way, 'mother me.' I would need to choose if that was the life I could lead, and if so, there would be a lot of joy, but also tears.

She went on. "Charles is also a part of your past lives. He was in a position of service to you as a queen some lifetimes ago. He still finds himself wanting to be of service. This confuses him. You were the one he never really reached in his quest for a deeper and lasting romantic love, and so he still holds you in that space—out of reach, the one he cannot have."

After a pause, she said, "But there is another. Someone you will meet soon, when you least expect it. You must go home and write details of the man you would most enjoy living with. You must draw him to you."

So here it is, Diary—my perfect man:

- Tall — around 6 ft anyway

- Athletic— great physique - - cut muscles, likes to play sports

- Interesting eyes — windows to his soul

- Independent, like me

- Loyal — will not have me guessing about his heart

- Fun-loving and adventurous

- Someone I can be quiet with — no words, yet feel comfortable

- Compassionate — of service to others

- Educated

- Good listener

- Good hands

- Great butt in jeans (shallow, but true)

- Spiritual seeker, like me

- Handsome

- Good father (potential when I meet him — not actual father yet)

- My head fits on his shoulder when we dance

- Good lover

- Good dancer

- Someone I can work with side by side, maybe share a business with some day.

Wow, now that I have written this, I see that I am only partially describing Vito and I am unresolved about Charles.

Damn it.

My impending marriage to Vito brought a flashback to feelings I'd had before my first wedding—back to 1975, the worst of all fashion years. It was the year of The Wonderbra, lycra leggings and Reebok sneakers, long nylon paisley print tops, big hair, black eyeliner and, oh, let us not forget Saturday Night Fever, which gave us polyester leisure suits and Cuban-heeled boots. I probably should have paid more attention to the songs I was singing in my car that year like "My D.I.V.O.R.C.E." by Billy Connell and "He Don't Love You Like I Love You" by Tony Orlando and Dawn.

I did realize—but not until three weeks before my first, Big Ole Southern Wedding with nine bridesmaids, punch, cookies, and little green mints—that I was making a mistake. I'd sat in my bathtub at home staring into space, with a yucky feeling in my gut, but I was committed. I was in motion—the featured bride in the newspaper's June Bride section. I had to go through with it. That's what good, Southern girls do, right?

I was feeling hesitation about getting married again. Fortunately, I faced this decision a decade older—and a bit wiser. I went to pick up the invitations about a month before the Memorial Day wedding. I took them to my car, buckled myself in, and started weeping. I grabbed the box of invitations, got out of the car, walked back inside to the lovely cashier and instructed her, "Please hold these for a week and if I am not back, toss them." Then I drove two hours west on I-40 to Winston-Salem, where I entered the foyer of a home I had decorated and looked into the face of the handsome Italian man I had spent much of the past six years with. We wept together and talked—and talked and wept. He convinced me to push back the date. I went to the guest bathroom and splashed water in my face. As I turned to get a towel and my bearings, I saw a pink Daisy razor on the tub. I didn't use Daisies. My head started spinning. His three sisters had not visited in the short time between my last stay there and that afternoon. I walked out into the hallway clutching the razor, and his smile faded. He didn't say anything. He didn't need to. This was the confirmation I needed to move on. I half-heartedly laughed as I mock-punched him in the arm and started weeping from relief and the realization that my future plans had just changed again, and I had no idea what would happen next. He started to offer an explanation, but I held my hand over his lips. I hugged him for a time out of time, picked up my things and left.

Driving to Mom and Dad's house, I thanked God I had known Vito, and that he had been with me on this road to a new self-awareness. I had no idea what was next in my life, and more than anything else that rattled me. I hated being clueless—not knowing. I thought at the time that Charles might be an answer. Mom greeted me in the driveway, looked at my tear-stained face, walked back to the kitchen and started cooking. It was always our best therapy.

While the dinner simmered, we went outside to shoot basketball for awhile, just her, Daddy, and me. We played H-O-R-S-E—follow the leader, miss a shot, gain a letter, until I didn't feel like shooting anymore. I cried and shot, missed the basket and laughed. I lost every game. Then we sat down to her southern fried chicken, mashed potatoes with peppered milk gravy, black-eyed peas and corn with Daddy's hot peppers cut into small bits and sprinkled on top, and a pear salad with cheddar cheese topped with a fat-filled dollop of mayonnaise. This was "my" meal. This was my place . . . Welcome . . . with its toothpicks, racecars, sprayed hair, and milk gravy.

All would be well, I reasoned as I closed my eyes to go to sleep in the small bedroom still decorated with red sponge paint on the white walls, a reminder of the nights I had spent there, dreaming of heaven. All would be well, indeed. It always was.

Hmmmm. . . I guess it always is.

February 15th, 1985

Dear Diary,

About last night –

As I settled into the bedroom of my youth, I surrendered in prayer, "Thy will be done and thy will be fun, God." On the drive back to Raleigh, I passed the turn to Maw Maw's house. The song, "It's Alright, have a Good Time" by the Impressions started playing on the radio. Tobacco aromas filled the car, and I laughed out loud.

I don't remember all the lyrics, but the essence of the song was that things were going to be "Alright," regardless of how bad they seem at the time. So if you wake up feeling sad, realize that you've gotta have hope that something good will "come to you."

That song has shown up at other times in my transitions. It apparently carries a message for me about trusting and having fun. I have learned that when I love what I am doing, when I am having a great time, then I seem to attract more of what I want. So I pay very close attention to where the music shows up for me- and where I become more attractive to those things I really want.

Synchronicity

April 13th, 1985

Dear Diary,

A Pig Pickin'! It's a Saturday, and I am in town, and there is a Pig Pickin' in the neighborhood. I am in Hog Heaven! Slow-roasted pig cooked outside on a pig cooker all day long, with hushpuppies and cole slaw, hot sauces and roasted potatoes. Nothing could be finer in Carolina! (I cannot believe I just wrote that.)

Okay, I have traveled so much and spent so many weekends away that I have totally missed making good friends here. Tonight I met some really cool people, especially "Cute

Boy," with the great legs and interesting eyes — one brown and one blue. I called Dana and told her to get her butt over here. I introduced her to "Cute Boy" and the three of us spent a lot of time talking about his Peace Corps service in Sierra Leone. He said he left here in hopes that when he returned, 'Disco would be dead!" He promised us he cannot dance, so I can check him off my list, but he is interesting - Lives with his sister right around the corner and likes to cook, so we may share a few meals.

Dana left late tonight after giving new "Cute Boy" her phone number. Maybe that will be a good match.

Cute Boy's name is Barry. Dana told him I am engaged, even though she's clear that I am not. Probably her signal to stay away. Darn it. She is moving to Boston this summer. I'll miss her, miss having people mistake us for each other. She's a little taller, but we wear the same style, have the same highlighted hair and brown eyes — same shoe size, 5 1/2. Shopping with her is like a fashion tug-of-war. We have to run to the racks to make sure we get first choice. We shop the outlets together. We are both so cheap when it comes to paying for stuff. I am saving for a house, and she is saving for her move to the big city.

Vito has been calling. He wants to come talk, so who knows what will happen with all these relationships? I guess it can really be kind of fun not knowing where the road will lead.

When do we learn to trust our hearts as we make life choices? I am not sure, but somewhere along the line, I did. I stayed friends with those I invested time in getting to know as intimate partners, but I started searching for more meaning in my relationships with men. I needed depth, reflective conversation, and to be cherished.

I learned that I have a capacity to love people in ways that can sometimes wear them slam out. I also learned that it was important to keep talking. Above all else, I had to keep talking through the things that hurt me, excited me, and made me wonder. I had to learn to let go of those relationships that kept me from being my boldest self, the daring one. But I had to dare to scare Barry before I discovered that!

Cocoon

May 20th, 1985

Dear Diary,

Well, I have just scared away my new friend, Barry. We went to the movies to see "Cocoon," the new Ron Howard movie about ETs, as our first "date". I loved it. On the way home, I told him about the event to call spaceships at Hanging Rock and also about the time when I was 16 that I thought I had seen one. He allowed that "it could be true - it would be arrogant to think that we are here in the vast cosmos, all alone." So I thought we were hitting a good stride. Then he got out of "Lipstick," my new little red Audi, and covered the 40 yards to his door in two giant steps. He never looked back. He either had to "go" really bad, or I have just terrified him with my story. Oh well.... He is spending some time with Dana too, mostly when I am out of town, and she says they talk about me a lot. In fact, she said last week, "He really likes you, DJ." I felt like I was in grade school.

Probably for the best that I just allow him to be scared away.

Note to self: Do NOT tell anyone else about seeing things—spaceships, psychics, rainbow colors around people's hair hats. It may all be total hooey, anyway.

It has always been a dance between two worlds for me, always active in some church and being raised Southern Baptist from the time I was 13 (as before that we were Church of Christ goers in a century old family church in the country) yet having this incessant curiosity about all things spiritual, the questions, and the mystery that beckons me to take a deeper look. I worked so hard to prove I was smart when I was younger, instead of trusting my intuition. I over-compensated at times when I just needed to surrender and stop naval gazing or contemplating life and just live it. This was one of those times.

Barry left flowers and a bottle of wine on my porch the next day. A friend in the advertising business who was traveling through from Atlanta walked in the door behind me and saw the gifts on the porch. "Somebody has an admirer," he said. I was shocked. Then I thought, well maybe there's intrigue ... and maybe he just had no bladder control whatsoever.

Home

September 12th, 1986

Dear Diary,

I found you while unpacking boxes today. You and I have just moved into a new home I built as an investment and more — a home for me. It's such a sweet space. There's a front porch, a master suite, cherry cabinets in the kitchen, hardwood floors, and a walk-in closet for all the clothes I am accused of having. I am now a homeowner and won't be shopping so much to pass the time. I have learned that we make 45 decisions for every square foot of space and that $140K house will cost somewhere in the range of $350K by the time I pay for it.

Barry is here much of the time, fishing at the small 12-acre lake which is the centerpiece of the neighborhood.

Dana moved to Boston. I obviously didn't marry Vito.

My Budweiser client provided a keg o'Bud for my house-warming party last weekend, and we roasted streaking southern oysters with bacon, butter, and garlic in half shells on the grill. He also used one of the Bud banners to make a sign for the oyster roast, "Get Slimy with DJ," which he hung between two trees, right next to the house. Lovely, I thought, as I parked the new Volvo in my new family neighborhood. The radio staff loved it when they arrived for the party, but one of my new neighbors commented "in jest" or so she said, about how she was afraid for the home values if I left the sign between the trees overnight.

I care way too much about impressions. I will work on letting go of those and just having a good time. And, most likely, I will shack up with Barry-man often and really give them something to talk about. Cohabitating could probably cause lower home values too.

"Bless their hearts. Bless their judgmental southern hearts. I will be a good neighbor . . . they'll see!"

Good to find you, Diary. Too long since I have written.

Ooh, this is when my rebel came out. So, I am daring. I woke up one morning after moving into the house and stopped caring too much about what people thought of me. I laughed too loud. I laughed at the wrong stuff. And while my clients had always taken me seriously enough, like the Bud client, they seemed to know they could play with me. Most of them had done that and I think that playing together served us. What a great time in my life. Radio days were adventure days. You never knew who would show up, or what would happen next. Mostly I loved the places radio allowed me to go on business trips.

Connection

April 17th, 1987

Dear Diary,

My HAIR is way TOO BIG, and Barry and I leave for Bermuda tomorrow. What was I thinking? I let young mister hairdresser talk me into a perm, since my hair was getting longer and the look was now fuller. He let me process for 25 minutes, and I ended up with springy curls. When I pass a mirror, I can't help thinking that I have a small poodle draped over my head. My hair seems to remember those Toni home perms Momma twisted into our scalps when we were young, and it just gets scared and screws itself into those same ringlets. Momma wanted us to look like Shirley Temple. I just wanted my hair to be straight as a stick so it would blow in the wind when I rode my stick horse made from a wool sock and broom *handle through the backyard. Now it is permanently damaged and I am entertaining 40 clients in the humidity of Bermuda tomorrow, where I am certain I will bloom like a Chia pet. Arghhhhh!*

Barry and I had taken the inspection trip to Bermuda in November the year before in preparation for entertaining 40 clients and their guests. We had a blast. We chose the meals, the excursions we would take with our best advertisers, including a day-long fishing trip and a dinner cruise. I think this may have been the place our lives finally intersected. I knew he loved me, but he seemed challenged to articulate it. I was convinced that if this wasn't right, it wouldn't work, and so had become more discerning and detached. "What will be, will be" had been my motto, so I allowed this to unfold...and I kept moving forward into the life I wanted—a home by water, a feeling of being settled, a place to entertain good friends, time with my girlfriends. I just lived one day at a time, becoming whole and comfortable alone. But I knew in my heart something had shifted and this friend would be with me in some way for life.

Church Bay

June 11th, 1987

Dearest, Beautiful, Magnificent Diary!

Today is my 32nd birthday! I have something important to share. I have to write it like it unfolded.

Barry had the Elbow Beach Hotel pack a picnic lunch for us on the second day of our trip to Bermuda. We went for a scooter ride, and when he saw a sign for "Church Bay" to our left, he almost threw me from the scooter as he turned in. "This is the perfect place," he said.

After we ate the croissant sandwiches with curried chicken salad, fruit cubes, and fresh-baked macadamia cookies, we talked for a while, congratulating ourselves on planning a lovely trip for the clients. I lay my head on his arm, closing my eyes, and this vision flashed through my mind of Barry proposing. Not a minute later, he said,

"This is the perfect day and the perfect place." He pulled a sapphire-and-diamond ring from his rolled-down sock (HIS SOCK!) and presented it to me. The only thing I could think was, "He is about to propose to me, and my hair is WAY too big. He left the USA hoping disco would die, and now he is about to propose to someone looking like a disco queen."

"DJ, will you marry me? Will you be my wife and live the rest of your life with me? You won't even have to change your name to mine if you don't want to."

I think I lost my breath for a moment. It was like I was watching a movie within a movie. — talking to myself about hair and what I was about to say and all the things that flashed through my mind. Did I hear a qualifier — "I won't have to change my name?" Was that a half-offer, or is he really scared I won't stick? I couldn't stop the questions rolling around in my mind. When I caught my breath, I looked at him inside out and responded, "Of course I will marry you." He slipped the ring onto my finger. It was sweet, very different than any other jewelry I had worn—a periwinkle sapphire sandwiched between two small diamonds.

Then I characteristically jumped up and shouted to the people below as I danced to the edge of a cliff over-looking the beach, "He just asked me to marry him!

Did you hear that people! Did you hear that fishes! Did you hear that seaweed! Did you hear that Maw Maw! Ha, Ha, Ha!" I couldn't stop laughing. He had pulled off a beautiful surprise.

"By the way," he said, "I asked your parents to bless our marriage last month when they visited."

"You did? What did they say?" I asked, as I considered that if it had been me in the same position, I wouldn't have had the courage to ask for a blessing for a woman who had been married before.

"They said. 'If it makes our girl happy, then we will bless it.' I think you might want to call them and let them know we are engaged."

"And Dana. Shall we call her?" I asked.

"Yes, and Dana, who was there from the start."

As we settled onto the scooter to leave Church Bay an hour later, I slipped my arms around his waist and he said, "We are going to do some great things together, you and me. We are two people looking at the world through the same lens. How often does that happen? This is going to be an adventure."

I held on tight.

Holding on when you have no control over the ride is a major part of the adventure in marriage. I didn't hesitate when he asked. I knew. A calm sense of peace and rightness fell over my body. I have learned to trust that sense of knowing.

He was a scientist with a Peace Corps background—not what I had expected; yet he matched every description on the list I had written in my diary years earlier. Well, almost every description— he really couldn't dance!

Okay, he could dance the minimal, the African dance to steel drums, so our outdoor wedding three months later was followed by a Luau with a band from Jamaica. As they played steel drum music, we danced and limbo'ed our way into the pool, where the entire tribe, his family and much of mine, ended up fully clothed in a synchronized water ballet.

We have learned to dance together with what life offers. Sometimes I lead, and sometimes I willingly follow his lead.

I knew him when we met. His eyes were the reminder for me... the invitation. I still hold on, but not so tight. No need when you stand side by side in a view of the world.

Expecting

January 20th, 1988

Dear Diary,

I cracked an egg on my pizza tonight and put it into the oven to bake. First one piece, slowly savoring every bite and then, like a crazy woman, I ate the entire thing. Knowing this was strange, even for me, I decided to buy an E.P.T.

Tra Lah—I am about to become a Weeble! We are going to have a baby!

I tied a yellow ribbon around the large appendage of the soapstone fertility statue from Sierra Leone and left it on the kitchen counter. Can't wait to see Barry's reaction. Ha!

This was the sweetest feeling in the world. Life growing inside me. Life the size of a tadpole just swimming around in creation soup. I was absolutely complete in that moment, and ripe with anticipation that I was going to give our lives new meaning with the gift of this baby.

Loss & Gain

May 23rd, 1988

Dear Diary,

I'm 16.5 weeks pregnant. We did not hear a heartbeat today. It was the second time in a week that I've laid on the table waiting for the thumps that should go with my expanding belly and heard nothing.

The doctor came in to let me know that there were two empty sacks where there should have been two babies. I have a couple of blighted ovum—just bags of fluid, but no babies left inside. It was as if someone had taken them out in the middle of the night. This was the most gut-wrenching news I have ever heard.

I have wept all afternoon, and it appears I will be in the hospital later tonight for emergency procedures.

Maw Maw, what happened to my babies?

"Oh, my Precious one, sometimes the body is prepared and some-times these spirits prepare the body. They will make choices to come to you in another way. Trust. You will be a mother. You will be a beautiful mother. All is well. They come to teach you and to share the light."   *"I love you," Maw Maw*

I will trust Maw Maw. I will.

Note to self: Maw Maw is now answering my questions??????

This entry was an awakening. This was the first time I had posed a question and had an answer show up as if I was reading a ticker tape on an electronic billboard—an automatic writing. There, in the midst of a tremendous loss, I started a new conversation with Maw Maw. While I worked through the suffering, a door had opened and I gained access to Maw Maw in a way that would be with me for the rest of my life. Yet, it felt too easy, and I didn't trust it totally until it happened several more times, a couple of years later.

░ ◊ ░

BOOK III
LESSONS

░ ◊ ░

My view now about
Lessons of Faîth

*When you were born you cried, and the world rejoiced. Live your
life so that when you die, the world will cry and you will rejoice!*
-NAVAJO CEREMONIAL BLESSING
(also attributed to other traditions, including the Sufis and East Indians)

I am not sure when I really started viewing things that happened
to me as lessons, miracles, or as grace, but somewhere, somehow,
it happened. I learned to see myself in Earth school, here to learn
with others whom I would encounter. Now, when things are working, I say a blessing of appreciation, and when they are not working,
I look at the situation to see what I can learn.

The Dali Lama wrote, "If you lose in life, don't lose the lesson." That is a big part of the journey for me. Everything has not worked out like I planned or dreamed. And when I have lost something, I have had the gift of a handful of spiritual teachers and guides, including my Maw Maw Precious, who are always there in some form, helping me to find my way.

It is when we learn to give witness to the daily miracles in our lives, to be completely present with the people, enjoying the day, tasting the food, appreciating nature, that we experience grace and pure joy.

□ ◇ □ ◇ □ ◇ □ ◇ □ ◇ □ ◇ □ ◇ □ ◇ □ ◇ □ ◇ □ ◇ □ ◇ □ ◇ □ ◇ □ ◇ □ ◇ □ ◇ □ ◇ □ ◇ □

Forgiving

June 30th, 1988

Dear Diary,

Today my boss called me into his office after everyone had left for the day. He was agitated for some reason and with a wild look in his eyes, he screamed at me, "We have a big budget to make this year, so I need you to give 110%. There is no way you can get pregnant again and deliver these numbers this year."

I felt as if someone had punched me in the stomach. I was standing up when we started the conversation, and then I was sitting in a chair, tugging at my skirt. I started trembling, gasping for breath. I held myself in a hug as protection, and then as deliberately as I could manage and with a voice that didn't sound like mine, I told him, "You have crossed the line. I cannot imagine how someone in your position could be so cruel after my loss. If we have to adopt children, we will. I was meant to be a mother."

I wanted to call him every bad name I could conjure up. I just thought it as fire came through my nostrils..."What a stupid asshole—a stupid, insensitive man," was the meanest thing that I could force through my mind. Somehow that anger catalyzed the courage I needed to stand up and walk out.

As I walked to the car, my knees buckled and I sat on the brick retaining wall next to the parking lot and wept. When I could breathe again, I made my way to the car and drove home. Barry took one look at my face when I opened the door and grabbed me in a hug. "You okay?"

I couldn't speak. I drew a bath in the master tub and lit candles. When I finally felt grounded in the water, I started crying again and related the story. My voice sounded primitive and far away. For a moment I could only grunt out the words between deep breaths, "I've just learned that people can be cruel beyond belief."

Before I could give Barry all the details, the phone rang. My boss was on the line wanting to speak with me. I shook him off.

I soaked until the water got cold, completing the story for Barry.

"You want me to go beat the hell out of him?"

"Yeah, great, and then I will get to visit you in jail. I can't even think about what to do yet. I need some help sorting through this.

I need you to be strong for me about this. Help me sort out the right thing to do."

He did just that. He settled me by asking a few questions. What else could I do? What else did I want? Should I talk with the owners of the station? He finally said, "You are a star, my friend. You don't deserve this. It will be alright."

I relaxed and sat down to write in my journal, my trusted friend. Barry knew to leave me for a while and busied himself around the house.

Ok—Guides, What do I do now?

"You learn the power of forgiveness. Begin with forgiving yourself for the loss. Then forgive the anger present in your family—it is that anger that will show up in every authority figure in your life, until you forgive them. Once you heal this place from your childhood, you will heal generations before you and that are to come after you. But you must begin with you. This was one of the lessons you came here to learn."

I am re-reading this "response" as I write. What is this voice in my head? Where is this writing coming from? I am trying to understand, Diary. Is this my grandmother's voice, my Maw Maw?

"Yes. And it is more. There are many spirit guides who will speak to you through your writing. You just need to suspend judgment and write what occurs to you as your heart opens to receive these messages. Drop from your mind into your heart and find the answers

to your questions. Stop trying to sort through so many questions at once. Just write your one question, and wait for the answer. We will guide your hands. We are always with you, only a prayer away.

Tonight, let your prayer be to release . . .

> *the disappointment*
>
> *the anger*
>
> *the distrust*
>
> *the fear.*

Tonight, just accept into your heart the love we send, the power to become one who teaches only love.

We are your soul group, your true family of origin, the Michael group."

This was the event that set my hand to writing what I have felt guided to write. This was also the first time I realized that I really did need to begin by forgiving myself, something I had never considered before. I never thought of myself as being angry with me, but I was. More than angry, actually, I was afraid that my "sins" in leaving my first husband, my promiscuity after that, my distrust of men I got close to, my leaving the church of my youth, and all the things I had packed into my mental baggage were going to tumble out in my marriage and keep me from becoming a mother, from giving my husband children. I was afraid that I would lose him as a result, although I could not bring myself to admit it at the time.

But this writing was the first valid instruction that forgiveness had a power to change my world—that when I forgave, I would actually heal myself and make room for something else other than a recurring lesson. It was also the first time I understood that most people "know not" what they do to hurt us, as we often "know not" what we do to hurt them.

And the Michael group. This was hard to digest, but inspiring—a group of angels assigned to me, to watch over me, to guide my work, my life, to intercede for me, to co-create with me. My first reaction was "Zowie! I wondered how many angels are in a group?"

Light Worker

June 15th, 1988

Dear Diary,

I took yesterday off and went to see Veronica, a massage therapist and naturopath who owns Health Ecology, a school of healing arts. Marilyn, my good friend and earth mother guide, (whose claim to partial folk-heroine fame was that she once drank Southern Comfort with Janis Joplin) told me Veronica would know what to do.

I told Veronica about the conversation with my boss the day before and she had me lie on her massage table as she began a guided meditation. With Native American flute music playing softly in the background, she took me into a deep relaxed state, using a breathing exercise and visualization of walking by a stream into a peaceful pasture, finding a resting place under a tree. Asking me only a few questions to prepare for the session, she said the following as I lay quietly with my eyes closed:

"You are a light worker and a way shower. When you do God's work in the world, you literally become a light, a beacon; and you will equally attract and repel relation-ships with others. You will be compelling to those like you and repelling to those who live in darkness, but need the light. When someone such as your boss feels pressure or is in his or her own pain, there are sometimes dark holes in their energy fields. Imagine a picture of an energy ef-ficient house—these holes are a bit like energy leaks. So when others connect with you, they are trying to fill the holes with your light. Sometimes they are graceful in the way they connect, and sometimes they are like vampires, sucking life force energy out of you. They are human. You are also human. Imagine what you want this relationship to be about, to feel like."

Silence filled the room as she allowed me to really grasp the image of what I desired. That image was one where we worked well together, respected and supported each other.

"Now, bless him. Bless him every morning and draw this image of good relationship into your mind's eye so you

can forgive him when he 'knows not,' and create a new and
meaningful way of being with him.

She kept talking in a soft hypnotic voice. And then in
a breathing exercise she brought me back to a more conscious state, and I released the emotional grief. I still
had moments on the drive home when I wanted to judge Boss
Man as mean-spirited and an idiot, but I caught myself
and did my best to stay centered.

I blessed Boss Man in a clumsy prayer in my shower this
morning, not knowing how to get started with this new ritual,
but wanting to give it a try. I went back to the station for
our 8:30 AM sales meeting. I felt peaceful on the drive
over. He called me into his office after the meeting to
inquire, "Who do you intend to tell about our conversation?" I explained that I had been hurt, and that I was
in the process of releasing that. My goal was to have
a good relationship. I think he relaxed.

We'll see how this all turns out. I pray for peace.

My mind went crazy with the struggle between wanting to
retaliate and wanting to rest in this more peaceful state of being.
I called an attorney and checked out my rights. He explained that
I had a case that he felt I could win, but wanted me to know that if I
decided to pursue that path, I had to be willing to change my life, to
go for total ownership of the company or to never want to work in
the industry again. That is not where I wanted to spend my energy.

It felt bigger than me and really awful to consider the possibility that this would be the right thing for me to do.

We found our way to respect over time. We went on with our business and developed a new level of appreciation for each other. I suppose we had been through a sort of alchemy. We both changed as a result—he was softer with me, and I became more direct with him. I hung on to Veronica's words, "You are a light worker," and reminded myself when I was upset that this required me to see the highest and best in others...the God-likeness in ALL others.

Later that same week I said aloud to Maw Maw, who always spoke from her heart, "Did anyone ever do anything to hurt you? How did you forgive them? How did you maintain a sweet, funny spirit?"

Her voice danced across my mind, and I wrote in my journal:

Precious One,

The world cannot take your spirit. You always have a choice about how you feel about people. Everyone you meet is on a journey to wisdom, to heaven. Being a guide requires that you release judgment and see their best. That is what the Masters do. When Jesus held others in a state of perfection, they saw themselves in the mirror of His eyes, and they became whole. The Buddha saw perfection in everyone and everything. These virtues allowed others to heal in their presence.

I am always with you,

Maw Maw

Shifting Perspective

August 1st, 1988

Dear Diary,

I have had a fever for a few weeks and have been in and out of my OB/GYN office. I finally called Veronica after going to the emergency room last night for two shots of antibiotics. I saw her today for a Reiki treatment, which she said would help me shift the energy in my body. I have got to get back on top of my game.

Veronica opened the door to Health Ecology today with a bow, reverently welcoming me into the peaceful center. Her serenity and light appearance make her work as a healer even more magical to me. A sprite, petite blonde, she seemed a goddess of all things feminine. Her face radiated a sense of peace and well-being, which I so needed today.

As part of the preparation for the treatment, Veronica explained, "Reiki is a Japanese word, 'Rei' meaning Universal Source of Spiritual Consciousness or God's Wisdom, and 'ki' which is Universal life force, the energy that runs through all living things. Sometimes the Asians call this 'chi.' The practice of Reiki is a conscious way to become attuned to this Source. Reiki treats the whole person, the body, mind, and spirit."

She continued with the story of Dr. Usui, "the head master or 'sensai' of a Christian boy's school who had rediscovered access to this ancient healing art. She said that Christ had used it, as had the ancient Asian masters, but that it had been lost in human awareness except where the healers had passed it on in clandestine ceremonies throughout the ages."

I asked why anyone would need to be clandestine in this practice, and Veronica reminded me, "Let's see, the possibility of being persecuted by those with strict religious practices is a strong motivator. Remember, Jesus was hanged on a cross for healing a blind man on the Sabbath. Revealing obvious power was—and still is—a huge risk. It is beginning to find its way into a more general acceptance, though. You are a healer as well, you know."

She moved her hands over my body, beginning with my head and moving through the trunk and arms, abdomen, legs, and feet. With her hands resting at times above my abdomen, I could feel a surge of energy and heat sweep through my body. I felt as if I were in an energy cocoon.

I could have sworn I smelled a hint of tobacco. I remembered the bee stings, and it became clear to me that Maw Maw was a healer for me, here, in part, to help me "remember" or reconnect with the essence of who I really am, and what I came here to do.

I attended my first Reiki (healing touch) Class two weeks later. Veronica began the class with the story of Dr. Usui. Seven students, including my girlfriend Marilyn, listened as we began to understand Dr. Usui's quest. As he was teaching theology at this Christian boy's school, the students started asking why there were many gifts of the spirit currently being practiced, such as speaking in tongues, writing, singing, teaching, but there didn't seem to be any related to healing. They wondered, "How did Christ do that?" Dr. Usui set out to find that answer. He studied at the University of Chicago for two years, researching western medicine—still not the right answers. So, he followed his guidance to travel to a mountain in Tibet and to fast for 21 days, to wait for the answer. He lined up 21 stones to keep his calendar of time. Each evening he threw out a stone to mark the day. On the very last day, when he had "given up," he tossed the 21st stone. In that moment, crystal bubbles containing symbols, the appearance of hieroglyphics, appeared against a dark sky and burst into his mind's eye. He waited until he had received all the symbols, and then he left the mountain top, praying gratitude as he descended toward the village below, although he had no idea what any of this meant. As he walked down the path, he stubbed his toe and reacted by grabbing it with both hands. When he did, healing energy moved through his hands into his foot. The toe healed in an instant. He made his way into the village for a meal. As he sat at the counter of a local diner, a young girl came from the kitchen with her jaw swollen, head tied in a cloth. Dr. Usui asked the girl's father, 'what was the matter' and learned that she had a toothache. He offered to heal her as payment for his meal. He placed his hands on her face, as he had done with his own toe and felt the warmth move through his hands into her face. He held the position until the energy subsided. When she felt better, he knew there was a powerful force at work; he had found the answer he'd been seeking.

The story continued with the lessons Dr. Usui shared with his students about the opportunities for healing and the responsibilities—the partnership between those being treated and the healer. He then found a woman to teach the practice and symbols. At the time, World War II was changing the lives of many of his colleagues. He knew, however, that this woman could keep the information sacred and move out of harm's way to Hawaii, where she could teach others.

The most significant lesson for me was learning to understand the simple principles of Reiki. My certificate was folded into my journal. It read:

Just for today—
> *I will trust*
> *I will do my work honestly*
> *I will accept my many blessings*
> *I will be at peace*
> *I will respect the rights of all life forms*

I still keep this certificate posted as a reminder that it is living each day, breathing in the beauty of each moment that ultimately heals us. The energy ran through my body after my first attunement. Surges of electric current swept through my body over 21 days, three days in each of the seven energy centers, or chakras. I could feel energy shoot through my hands as I practiced with other students over the course of the next few weeks.

Expecting

January 29th, 1989

Dear Diary,

Two weeks ago, I started craving eggs on my pizza again. So last week I bought the pregnancy test and it was positive. I held my breath until I got the official news today from the OB/GYN office. I tied a yellow ribbon on the African fertility soap stone's appendage again today. We are going to have a baby. Yipppppeeee!

I had never felt healthier or stronger. Nine months flew by. My job was going well – we were the top-rated revenue producer in the market. I felt the baby kick within the first three months. Strong kicks. I thought I would have a boy. I sang and played games by poking the sides of my baby belly, loving the movements when little hands would meet mine in the poking rhythm.

Childbirth classes were fun, but we only completed two before my water broke and it was time to deliver a baby. Fifty-six hours of labor with a midwife and then an emergency extraction left me hospitalized for five days. They said I almost died during the last few minutes as the doctor vacuumed her out. I pushed so hard I broke every blood vessel in my eyes and my face and the nurse hung on to me so tightly that my arms turned blue. I had delivered a baby girl. Everyone moved with her to the baby prep station, and I tried to get my balance, to push myself up and get a look at her.

Barry said, "Look, what a beautiful face, what a beautiful baby girl. She is ancient. Look at this old soul." But I couldn't. They had her wrapped up on the other side of the room.

I couldn't move. I opened and closed my eyes, but saw three of everything. Finally, a doctor came to tend to me. All I could think about was holding this little girl, our precious baby Jessie, in my arms. When I finally saw her, I fell in love in ways I didn't know were possible. At home, I looked at her in the cradle my dad had made for her and thought aloud, "Look, Maw Maw. Isn't she just the most precious little girl you have ever seen?"

"She is a miracle. Children are miracles," I could hear in a whisper across my mind. "She carries the wisdom of ages."

I didn't know at the time that this baby girl would steal my heart and teach me so much about perfection and patience; that is to say, "perfection is the miracle of having a baby and watching her grow– every smile, every new tooth, every finger painting, every sweet nap, every new word added to a tender vocabulary. Patience is a learned trait for those of us who have trouble slowing down long enough to focus our full attention on anything meaningful, especially the child in front of us, who is depending on us for, well let's see, everything.

So from Jessica, I would learn patience, how to become an advocate, and how to stay present. She said to me, when she was just five years old, "Mom, I like it best when I am the Mommie, and you are the kid." After I caught my breath, I responded, "Well maybe, this time our agreement was for me to take care of you—for me to be the Mommie and you, the kid." The notion that this was a possibility left me reeling. What if she had been my mom in another time and space?

I didn't know at the time just what babies do to take charge of our world, but she was there to teach me to put family first. She was the magic child, a bundle of beautifully packaged sweetness. I would pick her up even when she was sleeping, just to smell the warm 'sugar' scent that was always behind her ears. I could see her halo of light change colors when she greeted me in the mornings and when I arrived home from work every day. Light danced in her eyes. I knew she was old and wise, but I had no idea how much I would learn from being her mom.

She mimicked me in many ways. I would see her teaching dollies and stuffed animals as I had done with my siblings as a child, placing them in a row on top of her toy box and pretending to read to them. I would catch her hunting through my bathroom cabinets for finger nail polish when she was barely able to walk, watching every move I made as I dressed for work. She wanted to play with pots and pans when I was in the kitchen. She was the girlie girl every prissy southern woman could possibly dream of raising.

I was softer with her than I was in any other relationship in my life. If I was stressed, she pushed away from me when I tried to hug her. She reflected the energy I carried in my body. She was the center of my world, but more. She was my mirror. That was a big lesson.

Jess had given me a new club of women friends whose little girls needed play dates. She had given me the challenge of balancing a career with my new-found responsibilities, and for someone who got their juice from their work—I could have worked around-the-clock before she arrived—this was becoming a challenge, causing me to rethink my priorities for the first time in my career. I was becoming aware of the fact that all I needed to do to find out how things were going in my world, was to look into her face, to see the aura of light change around her when I was in the room. Happy kid, pretty lights!

Moving

November 4th, 1989

Dear Diary,

I have been offered a promotion. The company wants to move me to Charlotte to be the general manager of the oldies station there. Apparently there is a need to boost sales, and they think I can do that, given my track record in Raleigh. I actually thought I was going to be offered the reigns at WXYZ, as that was the first overture. Barry and I talked about it, and I think we are ready for a move. We are going to find a house next weekend. It's all happening so soon. I've only been back from maternity leave for a few weeks. I hope I am ready for the responsibility. No, I KNOW I am ready for this.

I called Veronica, who explained that we are moving into a year of "1," a time of transition or a new beginning. She explained that the digits of 1990, when added together, total 19. Adding these digits in turn ($1+9 = 10$), finally translates to 1+0 or a "1" year. Feels like higher math to me. She said in numerology the numbers are added together - reduced until they become primary numbers. There is a meaning associated with each number. A "1" year is a time of new beginnings.

Yesterday, three of my sales guys overheard a conversation I had with Marilyn at the computer station about nursing. I told her how I had heard a baby crying in the grocery store and my milk let down. The guys thought it funny to sit outside my office, on the floor, crying like babies. My milk let down and soaked through a royal blue, silk Gucci blouse. They laughed hysterically. Between the spit-up on my shoulder and the company jesters, it is time to dress in Mommie clothes and move on.

I LOVE being a mom more than anything else I have ever done. I have a hard time putting Jessie down. She is so sweet. Leaving her at a day-care center is tearing my heart out, but Barry is good about getting her early most days. His office is in the house now, and he works part-time at an environmental tech company. He has started a home based company called Capital Training Associates and was just hired by NC State to do a taping of his presentation skills program called Technically Speaking. It will be marketed through the university around the world. I think he will be able to spend more time with Baby Girl, and we can find a nanny once we move.

Barry is so cute with Jess. When she is not in my arms, she's in his.

This was a time of new beginnings. Transitions always are– the end of something, the beginning of something—the expansion of family, a move, a new job, new places to shop, the trials of finding the right child-care. I had no idea what I was in for, or the challenges I would face. I was simply itching for a new adventure, a new start. I had a growing awareness that my intentions were also at play. I could desire that something new happen, or simply want something when I was shopping or daydreaming, and it showed up. In this case, I wanted a new start along with more time for being a mom. Perhaps being away from the home office would give me that opportunity—taking charge of something bigger would give me some freedom. I was ready for a move and new place to play.

As I was on the way to Charlotte with the station owners, they gave me a pep talk about what I needed to say to get people pumped up. I had met the sales people before and really liked them. The station, which was about four years old, was close to break-even. I was going in to turn it around – to make it profitable, as I had done in my past. I walked in the door to the conference room, waited for the introduction, and then made a total fool of myself.

One of the owners of the company had told me to watch the movie <u>Heartbreak Ridge</u> before I went, so I would know that I needed to be "ripping off heads and 'pooping' down some necks," at least that was the point he made. But that wasn't my style. So, in a most-inauthentic way, I told the staff I was there to change some things. I dropped a long portfolio of Jessica's photos in front of me and said, "Baby needs new shoes." This got a few of the laughs I was looking for, but most of the employees were terrified. I was trying too hard to impress the bosses, to let them know that I could be tough and turn a profit - or get a new team. I didn't realize how close these folks were in relationship to their former boss or how much many of them respected him, given how his performance had been dismissed by the owners.

It was the worst performance of my life. When the speech was over, I retreated into the large office that had my name on the door as a welcome greeting. My stomach was in knots. I could only ruminate over how to clean up that mess. I walked back to the conference room and found the door locked. They had locked me out. The owners explained that this was the type of behavior they had seen and it had to stop. The sales team was having a meeting about me in a locked room. I wanted to get in my car, drive home, crawl in bed with my baby girl, and not do anything else for the rest of my life. I sat in the office waiting. Almost an hour later, they came out. Some were obviously angry. Others were tearful. I apologized. They were not the enemy, yet I had treated them that way. I had really blown it. They didn't trust me.

It took me the better part of two weeks to hold meetings with each of them individually, to get to know them and what they wanted, and to try my best to make amends from the tragic mess I had made. One by one they saw my sincerity and most started to come around. Three people left, either of their own volition or at my request when they couldn't move beyond the mistake I'd made. I hired new people and formed a team. Revenue was down, but it began moving up.

Getting child-care was a nightmare. The first two candidates we hired were young and didn't work out for more than a couple of weeks each. One of them took Jess to her boyfriend's auto body shop every day for a while, unbeknownst to us. A neighbor finally asked if we allowed her to take our child out in a car without a seat belt. I fired the young woman over the phone. She never came back for her last check and the conversation I wanted to have with her about responsibility. The last nanny was fine, but she was 70 years old and slept much of the time. I came home one day to hear 13-month-old Jess screaming into the monitor, "Come get me, Miss "B!" It was 5:30 PM and her nap had likely ended around four o'clock. I was hauling groceries in both arms and accidentally dropped a bag as I ran upstairs to get her out of the crib. When I came back downstairs, Miss "B" made a beeline for the door and said something about seeing me tomorrow. The bag I had dropped contained eggs, and they were all over the floor. I put Jess in the high-chair and started cleaning up the mess. The "F" word flew out of my mouth, and a moment later, I heard a little cherub's voice repeating it. I had no idea that all children didn't speak in full sentences by the time they were a year old. She did. She had spoken words since she was nine months old. A lot of years had passed between my early baby-sitting jobs and having a child of my own. I was proud of the notion that Jess could say anything she wanted. I was mortified that I had added the "F" word to her tender, young vocabulary.

"No Jess, Mommie said 'duck,' 'duck!" I screamed far too loudly, and she started crying. I picked her up and hugged her, raw eggs dripping from my hands. We had been in the Queen City for a little over 10 months. I was beginning to hit my stride at the station, but the toll on my family was not worth the price. I looked toward the ceiling and pleaded as if there really were a host of angels listening to my every thought, "Please get us out of here."

Three days later, I got a call from the owners. They were coming to see me. There was a hint that they were putting the station on the market, but I also thought they could be coming to tell me I was fired.

That same afternoon a man who owned a news service called me and asked if I would be interested in moving back to the Raleigh area. The heritage hot hits station was seeking a new General

Manager. I had learned through the grapevine that the oldies station was indeed on the market. They were selling my Magic. There was always "magic" in my life, even in the name of the station I managed, and I smiled as that notion dawned on me for the first time since I had taken the job. I was managing "Magic!" This call, "out-of-the-blue" was also magic.

It took the potential loss for me to realize that I had been the catalyst for this next transition. I had desired something new, a way out, a way to play more with Jess—it was my intention that had caused this door to close and another to open.

Looking up, I whispered into the receiver, "Well, of course!"

Two weeks later I made the announcement at the station that I was leaving. This time there were tears that I was going. We had turned the corner and I loved the team. I repeated the announcement at our client party, a silent auction that same night, and I received a standing ovation from over 500 clients and guests. I'd felt for the most part like I was just hanging on for dear life, but this acknowledgment gave me hope.

It was time to move on. It was indeed a year of new beginnings. I had the guidance of an Invisible Hand that had always been present in my life, even when I questioned religious doctrines. It was this guiding hand that would always give me the faith and confidence that I was OK, regardless of the circumstances. I had learned to trust. All was well.

One year to the day after we had left it, we moved back into our little house on the lake near Raleigh.

D. J. Mitsch
Dragon Lady

January 3rd, 1991

Dear Diary,

I am now called the Dragon Lady! When I met the new staff today at G-105, one of the morning show announcers pushed open the chartreuse door separating the AM and FM stations and said, "Time to step out from behind the ole green door and go meet the new Dragon Lady!" He looked up to see me walking with the publisher of the newspaper and the company's senior executives, and his face turned purple. I burst into laughter, held out my hand in greeting and remarked, "I see my reputation has preceded me."

He may never be the same.

Tonight the company gave me a reception at the City Club. Newspaper execs and the radio staff were all in attendance. The creative services group had produced a version of an old Bing Crosby and Bob Hope movie—they called their adapted version <u>The Road to Radio</u>. They had dubbed over the voices to mimic the publisher, the interim manager and me. The female star of the film, Dorothy Lamour, played me. It was hilarious!

As Maw Maw would say in her most southern voice, "Honey, you have landed in a "pot of jam," which was her way of telling me that things were going better than I might imagine. The only place to go from here is up, and apparently I have a great staff, a creative group in place to do just that.

The publisher, Rick, is a fabulous boss – six kids, smart, supportive, and he drives a blue Corvette. "Daddy time with each child," he justified, when I asked about how he could get away with that. He and the assistant publisher, Dave, who served as the interim radio manager, have given me a new start. I learned today that I am one of only an estimated dozen or so women in the country who run radio stations. Who knew? Rick left me in the old newspaper office with these words, "Just manage your inheritance well and this should be a breeze for you."

Thank You Guides – Thank You Maw Maw – Thank You God. Thank You for bringing me home!

I learned a lot from my mistakes in Charlotte. Before I walked in for my first day at G-105, I knew everyone's name and position, and I had listened to stories of their successes from Dave. I knew the stations had lost $750,000 the year before, so I also knew they needed some leadership, and they seemed open and ready for change. I met with everyone personally the first week and listened to their hopes and dreams. The guys on the Big Band AM wanted to change the format to News Talk and Sports. I asked how long that would take to do since the station had produced paltry $40,000 total revenue the year before. They said "a week" and I gave them permission to do it.

There were so many things that were easy about this. I hired Steve McCall to manage sales. He had been an intern out of Wake Forest University at my first station management job in Winston-Salem, and I had taken him everywhere I went with the exception of Charlotte. We had worked together for close to 12 years. I knew this would also be easy for him.

□ ◇ □ ◇ □ ◇ □ ◇ □ ◇ □ ◇ □ ◇ □ ◇ □ ◇ □ ◇ □ ◇ □ ◇ □ ◇ □ ◇ □ ◇ □ ◇ □ ◇ □ ◇ □

Serendipity

February 14th, 1991

Dear Diary,

Today I hired Sharon Crone, a woman who called me just before I left Charlotte and said she had been told we were supposed to work together, that our radio receivers were tuned to the same frequencies. She called last week and told me again, "I am coming to work for you. When can I interview?" When she sat down in front of me, she looked at me in a way that made me feel odd, as if we already knew each other intimately. Maybe it is because she is also a southern girl. She also said she had seen a psychic in Memphis who told her I was going to move back to Raleigh and to just wait a few months for me to make that move and then we would be working together. So she waited and moved back to town two weeks ago, "knowing" she would be working here. She is definitely on the same wavelength. A former "Corn Meal Muffin Queen," she trumps my Future Farmers of America Sweetheart title.

Her sharing that story was pretty much all she needed to say for me to hire her. Thank goodness McCall liked her too, since I leave the final decisions on staffing up to him. She also has a brilliant track record in sales, so she's a safe bet.

Sharon and I are going shopping tomorrow. For her interview, she wore a jacket that was too big, with 80s-style shoulder pads. The other sales reps, who often likened themselves to female fashion police, let me know that she was a "cute gal, but needs to update the wardrobe — shoulder pads way too big." I am toying with whether to let them know about her "Corn Muffin Queen" status.

I never really need an excuse for shopping, and that will be my first order of business tomorrow. I love setting priorities!

Tomorrow night we are going to have a station-painting party and change the old green door to orange. I hired a designer to come throw paint on the walls with my team so we can signal the changes that are taking place.

This place is a dump, and although we are planning to move, we will be here another year and need to do something to lift the spirits in the tired, old, newspaper press building. These walls have seen a hundred years of news stories and the birth of these stations. We've been breaking out the old LPs and 33 1/3 records from the Big Band era and putting them on canvas for art. Some of the art is really cool, and it gives us something to do with our hands while we recap the workday. It's kind of like back at the farm, working the tobacco at the tables when what we were really doing was storytelling. People just need to work with their hands sometimes so they can find a forum for dialogue and feel like they belong somewhere.

Oh — and this tribe has already made budget for this month, AND most of March's total is already in! Yeah!

I hired a contractor to help move the radio stations into a new building, away from the old asbestos-filled, newspaper building downtown. The new office was featured in Architectural Digest. It was stunning. The staff had helped design their workspaces, so it was also highly functional. I had a small corner office in the shape of a triangle that was just the right size.

Jess was happy at the local Montessori School. Barry was back into the groove with technology and academics in the Research Triangle Area. I had forgiven myself for the mistakes I'd made with people. All was well. That time of my life was the absolutely most fun!

I had almost forgotten how I met the lithe beauty—and my dear friend—Sharon Crone.

Growing up in rural North Carolina gave Sharon qualities I instantly recognized when I first met her. She was a southern belle turned career woman. She'd answered a call as a teenager to leave her own version of Welcome, another southern hamlet in North Carolina, escaping beauticians that teased and sprayed hair into an upright and locked position, the drive-in-movie theatres that were always months behind showing the latest releases, the tent revivals, and the greasy cheeseburgers from the local mom-and-pop grills. If a girl ever dreamed about wearing a Diane von Furstenberg wrap dress in the 80s, and I am sure the "Muffin Queen" had, then she would have to find her place in a city somewhere. We claimed it was fate, fashion, and a love of rock 'n' roll that brought us together, and we had become fast gal pals, the kind that have a way of knowing your story without you having to tell it.

Looking back now, it seems she was always a part of my life. It was hard to know where she started and I stopped. Over the next four years we would finish each other's sentences. We loved each other. Sharon gave me the most amazing gift—her essence and her story.

God, I miss her.

Close Encounter

October 8th, 1992

Dear Diary,

Wow, what a day. I just met the most curious creature. It's been a while since I parked myself long enough to update you, and I have so much to tell — to write. We hired a new morning show team, Bob and Mike. They are wacky, eternal sophomores, which they hate for me to call them, so I do it sometimes just to get a reaction. A top-rated morning show was the only thing missing in our ratings last year, so I hired these guys and changed out the midday personality to bring in a woman we renamed, "Madison Lane."

One of the cool things about bringing in new talent is they

don't know what they can't do. Today I tuned in as I drove my 25-minute commute after dropping Baby Girl off at Montessori, and I heard them introduce "world-renowned psychic Star Capehart, just back from a tour that included a sold-out show in Madison Square Garden."

When I walked past the studio on my way in the back door, I saw Star Capehart through the soundproof glass studio window. She looked a bit like an haute couture punk rocker I'd seen in visits to NYC when I was there on business and went clubbing before I was married. Her spray of bleach-blonde hair was short and spiked, framing her high cheekbones and wild blue eyes—Caribbean Sea blue, because of colored contacts, I think. All of this was a perfect canvas for the diamond studs that lined her right ear. She was dressed in a black lycra cat suit with a belt that cinched her Dolly Parton waist. Petite, she could stare me down from her perch on five-inch stilettos. It was too early for anyone to have painted on that much make-up, but she looked fresh and air-brushed. Her Texan drawl sounded like residue of southern whiskey and cigarettes, as she gave the audience readings with a raspy laugh:

She was a bit of a smartass, quickly rattling off answers to the callers' questions:

• "Okay, Honey, now you can find that wedding ring in the corner cupboard among the china, where your toddler kid hid it as he walked through the house saying 'pretty, pretty."

• "Listen, Sweetheart - your lost cat is curled up under the porch of a neighbor's house—do you call him Smokey?' I see you calling him Smokey and holding out his favorite Meow Mix, shaking the bowl like you do for dinner. He isn't really lost; he's just been on vacation for a couple of days."

• "So, Darlin', you are trying to get pregnant and make a baby boy? Okay – now listen to me. This is no lie. It has worked a gazillion times for my clients. If you will determine when you are first ovulating—buy one of those thermometers that indicates when you are just ripe for the plucking, so to speak—then buy yourself, or make yourself, a chocolate-malted milkshake, like the big ole shakes we used to get at the drugstore counters, not a sissy shake like Burger Whopper sells. Make sure it has malt in it. Drink that and go do the wild thing, then hold your legs in the air for about four minutes when everybody is through, and in about 40 weeks you will have a baby boy. I swear by this recipe!"

• "Doll, listen up. If you have to ask the question about your husband cheating, he's cheating... and I'm getting the first initial of the first name, 'her name starts with an S, like 'she – issss- as – sssslick-as –a-sssnake 'S! "

I walked slowly to my office, stopping to greet McCall. Steve is tall and energetic. His devout family background gives him a sense of obedience and innocence we all find inspiring, and I can so relate to his sensitivities about religious traditions. I still hide our beer and wine in a cooler when my parents come to visit, keen to their judgments about how a "good girl" should behave.

This morning's radio show was unsettling for him. I thought he might feel the need to go ask for forgiveness somewhere just for listening in.

"Geez Boss, you think she is the real thing? She is scaring me."

"Scaring you? Making you think there is more to this game of life than what we know?"

"No. Well, maybe," he boy giggled. "More like scaring me because—what if she can read minds?"

I couldn't resist the opportunity to tease him a little.

"Are you afraid she's going to go poking around in yours? You, my friend, have nothing to worry about. Not much going on in your head but making that very large revenue budget this month."

I knew, however, that his questions and concerns would likely mirror those of the other 46 employees and our hundreds of clients. We work in the buckle of the Bible Belt after all, and our traditions are tightly woven into a cultural and familial fabric.

As I walked to my office, I overheard the morning show's live feed playing through my assistant's speaker phone. Bob was saying excitedly, "Well, it appears that one of our callers this morning has confirmed Star Capehart's legitimacy. Linda, you say you found Smokey?"

"Yes, I went out calling him, shaking his Meow Mix like the psychic said to do and he came running through the back yard. Thank you so much," she almost whispered, clearly close to tears.

"Superstar" Capehart had been a consultant on the set of "Ghost" and had other famous encounters she wove into stories, making her own brand of magic on the air. I left McCall with a nod and walked into my office with a cup of decaf and started reviewing the morning reports. Minutes later, Capehart was knocking at my office door, humored by the sign on the wall next to it that had been a mock gift from the staff when we moved the stations. It read, "The Dragon Lady." It had given me an opening to more than one interesting conversation.

"Dragon Lady — well, I see you know your spiritual heritage," she said in a booming voice. "You are a descendant of Asian influence and strong goddess energy. I am supposed to tell you to get in touch with that, and not to worry about losing this job, sweetheart. You had a guest in here a couple of weeks ago who was quite negative, and he was actually quite full of shit. Your guides wanted me to tell you that."

I went stone cold still. She was right about the guest. The week before I walked into the studios to deliver a tape during a commercial break and got blindsided. The morning show guest that day was a man claiming to be a local astrologer and intuitive author. He looked at me in the strangest way and said in an authoritative tone, while the show was in commercial break, "Missy, you had better get your revenue numbers up if you plan to keep your job here this year." Bob and Mike looked at each other, and then at him and started laughing, making light of his surprise attack, but I had left the studio a bit wounded that someone I didn't know would take that kind of liberty in front of new members of my team. Besides, we were beating the numbers. But I didn't argue at the time, I just walked out.

"My guides?" I asked her.

Capehart responded. "Yes. I had to meet you. You are one of my people. In fact, part of the reason I am here in Durham is to meet you."

I smiled a bit nervously, curious. Her energy was so big she filled my office and as she moved toward me I almost fell backward into an arty hand-carved chair. She picked up Barry's picture from my desk and said, "G-ur-lllll-friend, you have found your twin flame soul mate. His eyes, one brown and one blue, were your signal for instant recognition, probably the first thing you noticed.

Did he tear ligaments in his left foot when he was in the Peace Corps or playing basketball?"

Dumbfounded, I said, "playing basketball overseas in Sierra Leone, while he was in the Peace Corps."

Then she looked above my head, as if she were watching a movie playing, and blinked her baby blues rapidly. "And this little boy is not going to be waiting too much longer to join the fun. You know you are going to have a son too, right?" I just nodded, as if I did. "He will play finesse sports, baseball and something else with a stick." Then she re-directed her gaze toward me.

"I am going to spend more time with you, G-U-R-LLLL-friend. I'll be back tomorrow. We are going to trans-channel Nostradamus on the air. What a kick!"

She whirled out of my office.

I stared into space for a few minutes after she left, trying to assimilate everything she had said. Trans-channel Nostradamus? I remember feeling curious, but also wanting to be cautious. When would we take this too far for the people of the Triangle, the people I had the responsibility of serving? I was also responsible for protecting the license of the station. It occurred to me that we might be pushing that envelope with Star Capehart. And what about her "baby boy" comment? We had decided to have only one child, although I had a sense I would have two. (The Ouija board told me I would, right?) However, we were serious enough about family planning to have interviewed our friends who grew up as only children, and Barry was planning to schedule his vasectomy.

Sharon Crone strolled in shortly after Star Capehart left my office and said, "I've signed us up for two readings with Star Capehart this weekend at the Marriott." We traipsed around together on weekends, seeking spiritual teachers and retreats, so it was typical that she would want to have a reading, but this woman had already seen me in my environment. Capehart had my number in so many ways. This was different than the other times I had gone to see people who didn't have a clue about what I did or who I was. I could hide in their homes or offices. There was no hiding here.

I agreed to go with Sharon, having no idea that at the time the two of us were on our way into a spiritual growth spurt, one that would forever alter our lives. I went home and made a batch of fudge with pecans and ate the entire thing. My vision was impaired for the next two days from the sugar dump.

Nostradamus

October 9th, 1992

Dear Diary,

Star Capehart was back on the air this morning. I have to write this down — as much as I can recall.

She had set up an invitation yesterday for someone to be her guinea pig, receiving the spirit of Nostradamus, which she planned to breathe into her own body and transmit into the receiver, a detail I had totally missed. Star Capehart explained to the audience that she was trained as a registered nurse and she would be monitoring the breathing of Eddie Conner, a local soul intuitive who had volunteered to receive the spirit of Nostradamus. I could hear the blood pressure cuff as she pumped air in a consistent rhythm, while at the same time beginning a guided visualization and breathing exercise. I felt my eyelids start to droop and my breathing begin to slow down — then I felt the Lexus veer to the right. I turned the radio off, before I went wherever Mr. Eddie was going. Curious, I tuned in again five minutes later.

Bob was speaking, "Sharon has already started her hypnotic process, and we're going to be joining her in progress."

Star Capehart instructed Eddie, "I want you to relax your feet. Relax your ankles. Your ankles are totally relaxed. Relax your calves. Your calves are totally relaxed. Relax your legs. Your legs are totally relaxed. Relax your pelvic area. Your pelvic area is totally relaxed. Relax your thoracic area. Your thoracic area is totally relaxed. "

Bob: "My what? Look that up, Mike."

Mike: "Thoracic.....Thoracic. It's the age when the dinosaurs lived."

Thank goodness these guys were good at inserting some levity into the show.

Bob attempted to keep the listeners involved, "You are listening to psychic Sharon Capehart, and we're doing the first ever trans-channel transfer on the air. We're going to pull in the voice of Eddie Conner who is receiving the spirit of Nostradamus."

Star Capehart continued, "Think deep sleep. Deep sleep. We're going just a little deeper now."

Mike: "That's a Madonna song, isn't it? We can't say that on the air, can we?"

"You are going deeper...deep...deep...sleep. You're doing real good, Eddie. We're gonna go just a little deeper."

Bob: "She's trying to get him into a deep sleep because we're trying to get Nostradamus into an extended period of time. It would be cool if he could stay all day, have lunch — I wonder what he would eat?"

As I listened, my mind answered the question, "Quiche pie, sautéed fish in butter, fried potatoes with onions, and field greens. That's what he would eat. He loved pies and tomatoes. He loved tomatoes."

(Where the heck did that come from? Note to self: Stop thinking about food—your morning show is trans-channeling the spirit of a dead man—you are going to be in deep "doo-doo.")

Mike: "You know, I am wondering if we are going to get some grief for deliberately sending Nostradamus into another man's body. Is this legal in North Carolina?"

(Note to self: "NO, probably not in any state!")

I felt my eyelids getting heavy again, so I tuned out again for a few minutes to make sure I didn't go where this Eddie was going.

When I turned the station on again, I heard Mike's voice, beginning to sound a bit uncomfortable, saying, "He's gonna get the bends going that far down."

Bob: "Sounds like an ELO song—Going Down into the Deep, Deep Ole Southern Bends"

Star Capehart : "Now, Eddie, I'm going to take three deep breaths and I'm going to go get the spirit of Nostradamus. I'm going to pull him into my body. You keep breathing. Keep thinking deep...deep sleep. When I receive him, I will begin transferring him into your body. Now, concentrate. Keep going deeper."

I tuned out again for a few minutes.

When I tuned back in, she said, "Alright. Eddie. We've made the connection. Now I'm going to talk to both of you. Be very calm. Be very relaxed. Eddie, can you feel a presence around you?"

Eddie answered "yes," sounding a bit like a backwoods country boy—and very breathy.

"Very good. You're doing great, baby. Nostradamus, can you hear me?"

Nostradamus answered, "Yes," coming through Eddie but in a deeper voice that was much stronger and deeper than Eddie's had sounded.

"Very good. All right, now hang on to him Eddie, okay? He's very comfortable. His energy is positive. That's it. Don't fight him. You're doing great. It's okay. Nostradamus, have you met Eddie?"

"Yes."

Capehart: "Good. Okay. Very good. Do you mind if I ask a few questions? I promise I won't keep you long. Can we ask you some questions?

"Please do."

"Okay. Hang on to him Eddie, you're doing great. Okay, Nostradamus. Can you tell us how you received your prophecies, all the information in your writings? Were they channeled to you in some way? Did you get them from your guides? How did you receive your information?"

Nostradamus sounded European and very articulate. If voices were wine, his was a fine, rich Cabernet. It grew deeper. "Through dreams."

"Can you say that again?"

"Through dreams. Automatic writings. Voices all around me. Voices from the heavens. Voices from within. There are people now calling this time of awakening a New Age. This is Old Age information — ancient wisdom. This awareness has been around since the beginning of time. There is a very thin veil between planet Earth and the greater universe that is getting thinner. In the near future, many will see into other dimensions. The aboriginal tribes all over the planet, including those Native Americans who first inhabited this place, have always known how to access this dimension, take guidance from the angels and elders, so this is not new. You are in a time of awakening, a dawning."

"Can you tell us why you were such a hermit, preferring to stay to yourself as a recluse?"

"Society didn't take to me very well."

Star Capehart laughed, "I think I can identify with that."

Bob and Mike chimed in unison, "Well, we can certainly identify with that!" Bob mimicked Nostradamus' voice,

"It's a good thing there's radio, the theatre for ugly people so we can hide-out from proper society."

Nostradamus continued, "I was pushed into corners, and from there I would seek the love of God."

I had just pulled into my parking spot at the back door of the station, and I sat, enthralled, for a few minutes until Sharon Crone tapped on the window. "Let's go in and listen," she urged.

We walked together through the back door and stood at the studio window for a few minutes. No one looked up. We walked through the station, and by the look on the employees' faces, I knew we were shocking the system. "Great radio," I said. "You never know what these zany morning guys are going to do next."

(I was thinking at the time, "I really hope this flies!")

When I reached my office, I could see that the phone lines were lit up and the receptionist, the typically unflappable Demi, greeted me with her eyes wider than normal. We had ministers, priests, professors and avid listeners calling the station. Their responses ranged from love to hate. Some wanted more of this type of programming and some wanted the head of the manager who would allow this type of activity on the airwaves.

I fielded as many calls as I could, calming fears and inviting people to see the show as entertainment. The show was still in progress with Eddie or Nostradamus answering questions as fast as Star Capehart could ask them.

Then "the public storm (or as we say in the south "s-h-i-t") hit the fan!"

A minister from Durham called my direct line—MY DIRECT LINE (how did he get that?) and asked me if I went to church, and if I knew what it meant to be saved. I confirmed that I did and I was. He said he feared for my soul that I would allow something like this to happen on the air, and he asked for my minister's name. I gave him the name of our dear friend and minister, Pastor Richard, and then the daredevil in me took over. "Reverend, I happen to believe that God is everywhere, even in these studios with the eternal sophomores who are our morning show hosts. If you are personally offended by our show today, please accept my apologies." He kept hounding me, and I found my blood perking in my head, so I said to him, "Perhaps it would help me to understand who left you in charge of judging others? You have many choices in this area about what stations you listen to and who you serve. We also have choices. Perhaps it is time to consider that our guest today is either a brilliant entertainer, or has some gifts worth receiving?"

Then I heard myself say out loud, "Sir, you have not identified yourself, and I have many people waiting to speak with me, as you might imagine. See if this sounds like me hanging up." I looked down and the phone line was dead. I'm still not sure if the line went dead first, or if I hung up on a minister, but at the time, I was mortified.

"I hung up on a preacher, for crying out loud," I heard myself whisper in terror.

I tried to calm myself and get centered. I really wanted to tell him that I had been a youth leader and had served on a committee to build a church. I wanted him to know that I was a good Southern girl, that I loved sitting in church on Sundays, and that we had our daughter baptized in our Methodist church, yet I could not stomach his pompous attitude. Then the thought occurred to me, "If he is a minister from Durham, he probably knows my boss, and our 'abrupt conversation' might damage my good standing in this company."

"Oh, Lord!" I said to myself. "What if he IS my Boss's minister? He did have my direct number, which is dedicated only to my boss and a few others."

I could feel my skin blotching, even though I was calmer than I should have been. I smelled tobacco and rose water lotion.

Then the phone lines became overloaded and everything went stone dead. The electrical system was overloaded and we were off the air for a few seconds. The phone lines dropped the remaining callers, and the lights went out over most of the computer workstations.

I picked up the phone to call Rick. No line. I held my breath on the way to my car and as I picked up the mobile phone. When I reached him on his emergency number, he immediately said, "Great radio, DJ. You've got them talking around here. I loved the show yesterday; we've decided to try that malted shake trick at home."

I started breathing again. He went on to tell me that everything was fine, even as I shared my fear about the minister with him. "It seems that he got what he deserved. DJ, I've seen you exhibit your personal faith in the way you lead others, especially in fairness with your team. You are a world-class leader, my friend. I am not worried about your soul at all——your soul is just fine. You probably gave this minister the gift of reflection if you did hang up on him. Is there anything you want me to do about this?"

"No. Thanks for your support. Just be aware there could be some fallout from a pulpit or two on Sunday. Let the shareholders know too, so they can support us. That's all. Thanks for what you said about my soul. That matters to me."

The radio station was on air again, and I saw that as a sign.

Secure in Rick's affirmation, I sat and stared into space. Sharon Crone came looking for me minutes later with the update, "Phones are back up, and they are ringing off the hook. I just cancelled our lunch plans."

Gosh, that day was like traveling through space in the center of a tornado. It swirled around me, and I really felt as if I were in two different people, one just an observer and one smack dab in the middle of all the action. The writing continued.

So Diary, (Maw Maw, Angel Guides, etc.)

What is so threatening about a psychic?

"Precious One"

"Sacred" is only a transposition away from being "scared."

Those with sacred gifts often shake up the molecules and scare others, awakening the psychic part of anyone tuned in to this continuous flow of information and energy. Most people are not ready to live with their intuition so sharply attuned. They are afraid to let go of what is comfortable, and they are afraid of the unknown. Some are even addicted to their pains, to their sleepwalking state of being.

The one you call Star Capehart, takes her direction from the spirit world and she risks, often invites, having others shun her. You will find that this is a natural reaction to the words of Spirit. It has been so since the beginning of time, when man began an evolutionary process on Earth. People fear what they cannot control, even their own thoughts and truths. People shunned Gandhi, Confucius, the Dalai Lama, Martin Luther and Christ, so modern mystics are in good company.

When the time is right, humans in every culture will become overtly mystical again. They will trust the magical connections to us and create from intention, thoughts, and dreams. It will be accepted. People will give up on the notion that their way is the only way and become tolerant about many systems of belief, until there is only trust and collaboration. Out of need, people will begin to share resources. There will be only man serving man and the planet, not man controlling man or the Earth's resources for personal wealth or power. There is always enough on the mother Earth. Psychics will help direct and guide those wisdom workers who will awaken the larger population. They are the torchbearers lighting the way for others to follow. You will find psychics at every level of leadership.

You are a torchbearer and have psychic gifts. Anyone you encounter and befriend also has these gifts and this access. There are no mistakes in your connections. People draw you to them for this conversation, just as you draw closer to them — and that instant connection creates the space for a new level of consciousness and miracles to occur.

You and your people opened a cosmic keyhole today in the area. There were people who listened and needed to hear the words that were spoken and to have this experience—people who needed to *"re-member" who they are. It was no mistake that you came to manage these frequencies. It was part of your spiritual agreement, your contract. And the next steps you take, the next decisions you make, are also in part predestined and ready for you to step into, if you choose. We will keep opening the doorways for you. Know that some doors will not appear to be doors at all, and that you will always have a choice. We co-create with you. Also, know that we are always only a breath away.*

"It's all right; have a good time!"

Maw Maw and your other Spirit Guides!

Sometimes they sign off "your guides" and sometimes I actually get names. Sometimes it's just Maw Maw. I am not sure when things clicked, but at some point I simply stopped questioning. It must have had something to do with my dear friend Sharon.

Star Capehart came into my office later that morning with Eddie Conner in tow. He was still wrapped in a couple of blankets, as his blood pressure had dropped quite low and his skin was cold to the touch. When I shook his hand, it was like an ice cube. She introduced us, and I felt something familiar in the way he spoke. I think it was partly because he sounded like my country cousins and friends from the heart of Welcome, but there was something else. He was pure light. His eyes were pure, dancing, blue light . . . familiar, wise eyes.

The noise had stopped on the phone lines as Star Capehart started the conversation, "Gurllll f-r-i-e-n-d, I thought you were going to catch Nostradamus this morning. Good thing you tuned us out."

Again, I was amused and curious. She continued, "You and I worked together in the last phase of Atlantis, when humans finally destroyed the experiment. There were 13 light workers who kept the sacred energy center operating until the final days when the cylinders of light shifted and sunk the place. You were one of those 13 light workers, or temple workers. We reincarnated in this space and time with similar features so we could recognize each other and prepare to raise the energy cylinder.

I have seen you all from the astral plane. It is time for us to calibrate Earth's frequencies again as we move through the planetary shifts, so I will be connecting you all as I find you."

Now, remember that I had a Maw Maw who could see me inside out and share dreams with me, and I had seen a spaceship probe. So, it didn't frighten me so much to think that I might be a part of the raising of Atlantis while Star Capehart was in front of me, but then I remembered the excruciating conversations with those who wanted to have me removed from the planet earlier that morning. When she left my office, I was clear this was one story I would just keep to myself, and share only with my friend Sharon and a couple of those other girlfriends who were on a spiritual and inquisitive journey too. I would have to think about how to share this with Barry, who still held me at a distance in some of these conversations.

When Star Capehart left the office, Sharon came in and sat at the round, granite table. "Well, what did she say?"

I related the story.

Sharon laughed her signature belly laugh – the contagious, very loud, from-her-toes, girl cackle guffaw – and said, "Well, Dragon Lady, it is about time you get who you really are!"

Holy Moly! What if this Star Capehart woman is a loony bird? I believed her then. I had a sense that what she said was true. It made me feel excited to think I tended the energy cylinders in Atlantis. God knows every Southern girl wants to feel "special." But I stopped and started mentally questioning, "what if it turns out that she is just full of crap?" What if she took people down a path they weren't ready for out of some need to create a following? How can we know if any of this stuff is for real?"

It was at this point in time that my gal pal conversations with Sharon evolved into a steady diet of spiritual dialogue over lunch at the Dancing Moon and Ninth Street bookstores, as we read aloud from books that sparked us to a fuller awareness that there really is more going on than we had ever considered. Something Star Capehart did—maybe just the questions she made me consider in my own mind—caused me pay attention, seek to understand more of what I had previously held as possible. Still, I found myself wondering more than once, "What if there's no more to it than this? What if this is it...we come here, we live, and then we die, and that's it? What if the Baptists are really right – we live, we die, we go to Heaven if we are saved? What if others are right – we live, we die, we live again, we die, and so on, as our souls evolve toward heaven?"

Inklings

October 11th, 1992

Dear Diary,

Star Capehart's energy seemed less intense or frenetic for my session today than when I had met her in the radio station. She opened the session calmly, calling on my angel guides to assist with information for my highest good, as she guided me into a deep state of meditation with breathing instructions.

"What's on your mind today?" she questioned.

"Let's see—I want to know that my job is not in jeopardy because of what we allowed to take place on your morning show."

"Okay, Sweetheart, I understand that you need to learn to trust me. What scares you most about the show?"

"I love my job. I have the best gig of my entire radio career. I am allowed to lead and to compete with a ton of resources. I have assembled the most amazing team I have ever worked with. I am in love with my work—so, am I going to be doing this for awhile?"

"For as long as you truly desire—as long as this fits your purpose."

I was so relieved. I turned my thoughts to Sharon.

Star Capehart paused a bit before responding. "Hmmmm. Sharon is turning within. She will share her story with you...and she will need your love and support."

She kept talking, but the sensation I received regarding my dear friend gave me pause, and goose bumps formed on my legs and arms. The reading continued with me making up questions I already knew the answers to. It ended around fifteen minutes after it began. I knew I was other-focused and that I needed to find out what was happening with Sharon before I could even ask cogent questions about my own needs. I had gotten what I came for...I wasn't going to be fired.

I almost ran out of the bedroom to find Sharon and assimilate what I had heard. We said nothing for a few minutes as we made our way to my car. I could tell Sharon was ruminating over her session. "How did it go?" I ventured.

"Well," she said, as she glanced at her feet. "She's the real thing, I think. She had a hunch that there were cells in my body that had taken on a life of their own. She didn't name it, but I think she was trying to tell me that my DNA was reconstructing as more helixes were being added. She actually said some things I need to think about. She told me to allow Spirit to answer this call for motherhood. I asked her whether we should sell our house in Raleigh and buy some property we've had our eye on out in the country." She grew quiet and looked at her feet. "I think we should start thinking seriously about it."

There was a very long pause before she said something that gave me my first clue about what was really happening.

"Deeej, I need to go see a doctor tomorrow to confirm something I have had inklings about for a few weeks. I am feeling really strange about sharing what that is until I have more information. Can we stop this conversation for a while and let me think about this on my own?"

I knew my energy and enthusiasm could wear out even the strongest of my gal pals, so I decided just to be quiet until she was ready to share more.

"Of course. Want to go back to your car now?"

"No, I want a distraction."

I turned the car toward Cameron Village, our favorite shopping center in the area. It was time for a boutique fix.

I had an inkling, a strong sense in my gut, that my world was about to change. I just didn't know how.

Predestined

October 13th, 1992

Dear Diary,

Sharon heaved a guttural, primal-sounding gasp as she sat her boney butt on my lap in my office and told me, "The adoption fell through." She cried so hard that tears the size of ice cubes ran down the front of her white silk blouse and onto my arms before forming a pool on top of my desk. Two days earlier she'd loaded her red BMW with a brand new baby seat and diaper bag, put the final touches on the nursery she and hubby, Steve, had painted, and prepared for the drive to Tennessee for a private adoption. She is almost 40 and this was her chance to join the ranks of us mothers.

God, I wanted this baby for her, for them. She is so special, the wise one who provides perspective around the management conference table when it is most needed. We spend a lot of time together in our 70-hour-a-week jobs, and she is really more like family than a professional colleague.

She is totally brokenhearted, trying to understand how the 17- year-old birth mother could have decided to give the baby to a couple who bought her a Pontiac Firebird. I am angry with the faceless parents who would exchange a car for a baby. There were no right words to say, only kisses on her cheek and hugs to let her know I love her.

We brewed some herbal tea. Unusually silent, we left the studios and offices through the back door to get some fresh air. We walked arm in arm into the woods surrounding us. Bluebirds and cardinals chirped happily. The sun peaked through the Carolina pines.

"God, I love the beauty of the woods," she whispered. "Look at that cardinal. Have you ever seen one so red? When I was a kid, I used to think that birds took messages to God—and to Santa Claus. Do you think that birds talk to God?"

"Yes—

and to Santa Claus," I answered.

"I really want to share this with a family," she said quietly, as she turned to me, searching.

Why, Maw Maw?

"Sharon is a teacher for many, Precious One. She agreed to live with some big challenges so a host of people could share her story, learn from her. In some ways, this is her wisdom journey. In some ways, it's yours.

You two agreed to meet before you entered this earthly kingdom. You sat in a circle on this side and took on spiritual assignments— your lives are woven together. Just be the "Love" she needs now. Just Love Her.

Like I love you,

Maw Maw Precious

Neither of us had any idea at that time that she would be back in my office three days later with even more gut-wrenching news. She sat on my lap again, her fair skin turned red and streaked from tears, her light, ash-brown, wavy hair framing her beautiful, but very, sad blue eyes. Her shocked husband, Steve, stood in the doorway, his tall frame filling the space, somehow knowing not to intrude into our sanctuary. She settled her 115 lbs onto my 110, and I wrapped her torso in my arms, anticipating more news about the baby. Her voice was almost gone, as she slowly and breathlessly explained, "I know why the adoption fell through."

Diagnosis

October 16th, 1992

Dear Diary,

She has breast cancer. Sharon has breast cancer. I sit here on top of my bed writing this and it doesn't feel real. Sharon came into my office with Steve this morning and explained that she knew why this baby couldn't come to her now. She has breast cancer—very advanced. She was given 90 days to live. Oh, my God, 90 days! She said the cancer is so advanced that the doctors are advising against treatment. I don't know whether to be angry or prayerful.

Something surreal, the energy of empathic pain and angst sucked the air out of the room when she told me. I struggled to breathe. I hugged her with every ounce of energy

I could muster. We wept together until there were no more tears. I am not sure how long we stayed frozen in time. It seemed an eternity.

When the tears were gone, she perked up, as if someone had just changed the music score of her life. She announced, "Girlfriend, I don't know what this life lesson is all about, but I am not ready to die. I haven't finished what I came here to do. Together, you and me, we are going to beat this thing, write a book, and be on Oprah."

Steve finally looked up, searching my eyes. His crystal blue eyes matched hers. I had noticed that before, but today they were the same eyes, soulfully looking for answers, shocked by the news of mortality, hanging onto the ounce of hope that this was a nightmare. Perhaps, if they could find something to laugh about again, the nightmare would be over.

I heard myself ask her what I could do for her- where could I start to help.

She was quick to respond with, "Well, okay. First, I am famished. I have been a vegetarian for what – 16 years?– and today I have a hankering for a Bar-B-Que sandwich with coleslaw, some well-done French fries, and hush puppies – OR- maybe I should have you buy me some shrimp and grits at Crook's Corner?" She had eaten nothing "with eyes" in all the time I had known her. Now she was talking about eating my favorite southern delicacies, including pig. Pigs definitely have eyes – big ones.

She was diagnosed on a Friday. On the day after the diagnosis, I recall the horrible feeling of just waiting. She was in and out of doctors' offices and the hospital for tests all weekend. It was the following Monday before I would hear from her, or get a real sense of what was happening.

Waiting...I seemed to always be waiting.

I didn't sleep that night, waiting for news from the visit at Duke Hospital. Steve called the next morning and said that Sharon would be in later in the day to wrap things up for a while. Her doctors would be sending her to the Cancer Treatment Center in Tulsa, Oklahoma, where she'd undergo a chemo-drip for seven days as a new experimental treatment for reducing the mass so the doctors could then consider surgery. The mass had apparently metastasized into part of her left lung and this would be the only hope for corrective surgery. She hesitated to tell me about why they had not found the cancer, though she had been to see the doctors about a rash on her breast and other apparent symptoms for the previous three months. Apparently, a breast augmentation from many years before had hidden the early signs of the cancer. The cancer was more advanced than the oncologists had anticipated.

She was resistant to discussing the augmentation with anyone else. Like many of us, Sharon had undergone a crisis in her life that made her question her beauty and out of a need for renewed self esteem had elected to make physical changes. I wondered at that time if that was a part of the grander design, or simply a choice she made—was she destined to this? Are there accidents that occur out of our choices to make changes to our bodies, or is this a predestination?'

Steve broke the endless questions my mind raced through by letting me know he would travel with her, of course, and promised to call to update me during the week.

I waited for her, knowing that we would probably retreat to my office for a quiet conversation about what she was facing. When she came through my door in the middle of the afternoon, she looked happy and fresh for someone facing the news of mortality.

She was dressed in a bright yellow jacket and white slacks, happy Sharon colors, and she had her sunglasses mounted on top of her head. She gave me a hug and asked if we could call a sales meeting at 4PM when the sales staff came back from their day of sales. Of course we would.

I recall watching her as she meticulously prepared the room, arranging purple leather chairs at one end of the forever-long conference table, closing her eyes, praying, and then smiling as she greeted each sales person, her colleagues and truest friends.

"I have to go away for a week. I have been diagnosed with breast cancer," she said in a direct, non-emotive way. "I will have a treatment to reduce the mass that seems to have landed in my chest and will be treated here at Duke when I return. I plan to be back within the next few weeks. Please take care of each other until I can make it back full time." She smiled warmly, allowing her colleagues to digest the news.

The nine talented sales reps who called her "boss" sat with their mouths open in shock. I watched their expressions change from disbelief to grief to acceptance, their minds working through many of the same scenarios I had worked through the day before.

"I want you to know that I am going to beat this thing and write a book about the experience... And be on Oprah. So none of those sad faces you make when something's really wrong, like missing your sales quota," she quipped. "If I am going to be on Oprah, then you better have made your goals so you can afford to go with me!"

There was nothing I could say to the group except that I would give updates as I received them each day. Everyone played along to keep things light, until Sharon left to catch her flight.

Then, like curious children, they followed me back to my office and stood in a half circle inside the door. "What are we going to do for Sharon?" they all asked in different ways.

"We are going to follow her lead.

We are going to love her.

We are going to pray for her in our own ways.

We are going to continue to make her work shine.

We are going to hold her in a space of total wellbeing instead of illness until she can find her way there. That is all we can do for her now," I heard myself say that morning.

And that is what we did for ten days. We waited for word. None came. I was half conscious and half praying as I attempted to stay focused. Everyone else was supportive in their own ways. It was a bittersweet time of concentrated attention to our spirits. Radio events – remote broadcasts, mall appearances, client sales calls - all took place in a routine way. I know I was there in body and mind, but my spirit was traveling back and forth to Tulsa, pacing back and forth between my physical body and hers.

I cooked and ate, and ate and cooked. Comfort food was different for me every day. I ate Bar-B-Que pork sandwiches and hot dogs all-the-way with a side of onion rings. I ate alone in my car on those days Sharon and I should have been together at the bookstores. I ate vegetarian Jamaican food from her local favorite with the sales reps. I made my mom's meatloaf, full of ketchup, brown sugar and mustard, with mashed potatoes and gravy. I grabbed McCall and took him to Sharon's favorite restaurants in Durham, those serving humus, salads with lemon tahini dressing, grape leaves and tabouli. We raised a toast of water with lemon and hot Ginger Spice tea to aid digestion in her honor. We ate - and we waited.

Healing

November 2nd, 1992

Dear Diary,

It's been ten long days since Sharon left for Tulsa. She came directly to the station this afternoon from the airport, dressed in a soft-pink turtleneck and black pull-on pants from LL Bean. "Comfort clothes" she often called them, when I would slip into Levi jeans and long sweaters to tote Jessica around with us on Saturdays. Steve escorted her into my office again, holding her right arm gingerly as he slowly stepped one small step ahead of her. I hadn't expected her to show up without calling, and I was unprepared for her ghost-like appearance. Her skin was a sickish grey, her once-beautiful, healthy hair much-thinned, her arms bandaged under the sleeves of her pink top, as she moved slowly across my corner office. She probably weighed fifteen pounds less than when she left. She appeared to have been in a prison camp somewhere.

I covered my mouth with my hand, my eyes welling with water, tears stinging the inside of my nose as I tried to hold back. Nothing was said as she made her way to my chair and motioned for me to push back from my desk. As I did, she slipped into my lap again, noticeably lighter and more fragile. Then she broke the silence with a voice too strong for her body.

"Girlfriend, I am not going to live like this. If it is time for me to go, then so be it. I am not going to lie in some God-forsaken place with no light in my window, hooked to a machine that is dripping painful poison in my veins so I can rot away without my family and friends there to be with me, eat good food with me, share my life and my hopes and my disappointments with me. We are going to find another way. I don't really feel it is time yet for me to go. Tell me about your energy work, the Reiki. I know you have a healer who works with you. Let's go on another journey together. Let's find a way for me to heal."

Oh my God, she is asking me to help her heal. Is that what I am supposed to do, Guides? Do I switch gears here and focus on this work and forget everything else I am doing now? How on Earth do I help her?

I remember picking up the phone to call Veronica's number right away. Sharon sat still on my lap, her head on my right shoulder, her face buried in my chest. Veronica answered her office phone and indicated something about sending energy right away and asked if I could bring Sharon to the center in a couple of days, after she had rested from her trip. I had said nothing about a trip, just a few words about my friend being diagnosed with advanced breast cancer. Veronica explained that Sharon's traditional chemo treatment had left her weak and she asked me if I could I bring her for some energy work. I was beginning to trust the vibes of intuition even more. I was feeling pulled into a vortex, knowing things without knowing how, something I had experienced many times since childhood, but the frequency of events were seamed together – and they were happening in rapid succession. My friend Sharon Crone seemed to be serving as the unwitting catalyst for my own personal journey to trust in it – the Source of all knowing.

I held Sharon for a few minutes after I hung up the phone, searching Steve's weary face for an indication of what had happened, some direction to take the conversation. Sharon broke the weird silence.

"Did you eat some Bar-B-Que while I was gone?" Her impish smile broadened as I shook my head "yes." "I know you did. I could see you from somewhere beyond here. You ate your way all through last week, didn't you?" As I gazed at her, I detected a slightly pink glow shining through the grey.

"I might have gained most of the weight you lost," I answered facetiously as I looked out the window, pretending to watch the birds playing in a nearby tree.

"Well, my friend. We have just entered a new place, a new space. It is time," she declared, with a wisdom that came from a soul journey I had not yet taken.

"It is time," I repeated, not really knowing what else to say.

Then, it occurred to me, as if some cosmic comic strip author had drawn a cartoon balloon over my head, 'She is the Crone, the wise woman.' We usually called her by her last name, but the irony has escaped me until now. With my dawning awareness I said to her, "Well, the next time you decide to come back to this planet a couple of years ahead of me, could you make sure you are a little more obvious with your lead? I mean did you plan to be the Crone for just me and a few other people, or are you fulfilling your destiny to be the wise woman for our entire tribe?"

"The tribe," she answered without missing a beat.

"Well then, you have some major work to do. Go home and get some rest."

Steve reached under her arms, pulling her gently from my lap to help her to the door. He kissed my cheek and held us both together to make sure she felt steady, and perhaps to find his own equilibrium.

"I'll be back," she said with an affected Pink Panther accent.

No belly laugh, but there was lightness and a picture of amazing grace leaving my office, a quiet strength that stayed with me in the most precious way that day and for so many more to come.

Miss Conception

January 1st, 1993

Dear Diary,

I wanted to eat eggs on everything over the Christmas holidays, and yesterday it occurred to me that it had been awhile since I ate pizza with an egg on top. I've been so occupied with Sharon that I cannot remember the last time Barry and I even went to bed at the same time. I swear if we are pregnant, our pajamas must have passed in the night.

Just took an EPT and it is positive. Oh my goodness. This has to be the little boy I was told I would have.

I think most of the time, women intuit when they are going

to be a mom. The blood volume increases, breasts become beautiful and the brain flies out the window. The emotions are raw for reasons other than too much stress over the holidays. But more than a pizza, I want hot peppers and tequila. Strange...

Guides, anything you want to tell me?

"Hello Miss Conception,

You have conceived a son, and like his sister, he is also a member of the Michael group. He is a teacher. Enjoy this season. Be happy, as he will be joining Jessica to bring you much joy."

You know who we are!

I loved being pregnant. The African soapstone was again decorated with a ribbon around the largest appendage and I waited patiently for Barry to come home from work and see our fertility symbol sitting on the kitchen counter. He walked around the corner into the living room, where I sat with an open book, and said, "NO WAY! -How?" After a pregnant pause, he asked in his most serious tone, "Are you sure this is my baby?"

I would have probably been angry had I not wondered the same thing.

"Yes, and no," I answered. "Part yours, part little angels, if you believe my journal."

"But when? How? Are you sure? I thought we had determined that Jess would be an only." Another long pause, followed by, "Did you say seed of angels? Have you lost your mind?"

"Tra-Lah! Maybe this is the son that will continue your family's name. Maybe this is the boy the psychic told me about," I playfully shouted behind Barry as he walked out of the room and down the hall. Apparently there is little consideration for our best-laid plans when it comes to some things. God knows I like to have a sense of control, though by this point in my life, I had pretty much surrendered to the notion that I had very little.

Discovering

January 31st, 1993

Dear Diary,

Today we started the Healing Touch therapy for Sharon.

We entered the lobby, with a large, beige sectional sofa to our left and artfully arranged water fountains directing the energy directly in front of us. Sharon inquired about the music playing softly through the sound system — ancient flutes playing something she said gave her goose bumps, our way of knowing when something resonated, or was familiar, in our conversations or experiences. We nicknamed this goose flesh "God Bumps." We continued following Veronica, and Sharon pointed to her arms. Gobs of 'God Bumps' covered her body as she perched on the table in one of the five treatment rooms. Without a lot of inquiry into the diagnosis, Veronica began a calm explanation of the treatment Sharon was about to receive. The practice of Reiki is a conscious way of being attuned to this source. Reiki treats the whole person, including the body, mind, emotions, and spirit."

She continued with the story of Dr. Usui, as she had done with me, and she answered Sharon's questions, which mirrored mine.

"You will discover more once you have the experience. Just relax and lie down on this table, and DJ will assist me as we begin your healing session."

Sharon laid on the table, and we bowed our heads to pray for assistance from her angels and spirit guides in the healing. As we held our hands a few inches above Sharon's body, the rays of healing energy moved through us into Sharon's body.

Veronica informed Sharon about what was going on as we moved our hands into the positions I had been taught. "The right hand is sending energy, and the left hand is in a position to receive the energy. Each person receiving a healing will pull through the hands of the healer only the amount of energy needed. In some areas we may touch your body; and in others we will work a few inches above your body, respecting Spirit and your body."

When I moved my hands inches over Sharon's left breast, the heat was almost unbearable. Energy shot through my hands, and my elbows began to burn. Confused,

I looked at Veronica to understand what to do. Although I said nothing, she understood what I was experiencing and said softly, "Stay with the position until the energy wanes. Don't move your hands away yet." She placed her hands over mine and the energy was even hotter, but more manageable.

Sharon's first healing session took almost an hour and a half. Veronica stood at her head, and I made my way to her feet, as we closed the healing session, hands in the prayer position. Tears ran down Sharon's cheeks. She opened her eyes and looked at me.

"Well, I've been in hot water before girlfriend, but this is the first time I've been totally cooked," she belly laughed. "Does it always feel like this? I mean, the energy was hot in most areas, but it felt cool in some. It was really cool over my infected breast."

"Cool?" I asked, not letting on that my right hand and both arms felt as if they were on fire when we worked above her chest.

"Yeah, it was amazing. I want to learn how to do this. When can I take the class?"

Veronica told her about the next scheduled class and answered the big question about what causes cancer.

"Sharon, there are many reasons for disease in humans. Sometimes we come with a pre-disposed genetic program for disease, and we are to experience it and learn a life lesson from it. At other times, we take it on in order for others to learn from our experience of healing. And then sometimes, fungi or bacteria just find a way into our cells. Cancer is a term that is used very broadly, and it includes some fungal and other infections that have not been commonly identified or treated as cancer. Those things we can pick up from foods and environmental toxins. Louise Hay has done some work about the emotional and spiritual connections to disease, which you can read more about in her book, <u>You Can Heal Your Life</u>. I sell those and others in the front office. You will need to have faith that your body is responding to the treatments you receive and is fully capable of healing. You will also need to follow your intuition to know the best course of action. Sometimes a body responds to both Western medicine and Eastern practices, whereas sometimes it responds to the energy work alone. All of our collective intelligence about healing works together for the greater good. Quite often, it is what you 'believe' will heal you, that heals you."

As Sharon paid Veronica for the healing session, I remembered the first time I doubted my abilities to be a healer. After dinner one night, I felt no energy as I worked to heal Jessica from a nasty cold (one of the joys of having a child in the universal Petri dish called day care). I was feeling glum and was mentally questioning the power of Reiki as I went through the after-dinner clean-up routine. As I washed a heavy crystal bowl, it broke apart in my hands, slicing my right middle finger to the bone. I yelled for Barry, who had just put Jessica to bed, and he ran into the kitchen to see blood running down my arm and, me, obviously alarmed, for I realized a cut that deep would require stitches. He ran next door to get a neighbor to watch Jess. As he left the house, I held my right hand in the air, putting pressure on my sliced finger with my left hand. Even though I wasn't thinking about Reiki initially, my hands heated up. As I felt this energy, I bowed my head and consciously started the connection. I held my hand for the few minutes that it took Barry to return. When he rushed back into the kitchen, I took my hand away and there was a white gaping scar but no blood.

"Call the neighbor back," I told him. "I'm fine."

I continued to send energy into the wound, and the gash began to close. I found a bandage in the bathroom and placed it over the cut. In two days it was completely healed. "Probably not a good idea to question the gifts of the Spirit," I thought to myself at the time. I recall whispering, "Maybe this really will work for Sharon." I certainly felt the energy move through me when we worked on her body.

As an apprentice, my payment today was a bear hug from my dear friend, whose eyes were dancing with hope.

As we left the shopping center parking lot, Sharon squealed with delight, "I bet Eddie would love this stuff! Let's invite him to the class. If he can receive the spirit of Nostradamus, he can surely be attuned to this healing touch... this Reiki."

The Mission

February 4th, 1993

Dear Guides,

Reiki is an amazing connection for me. It feels like something big is happening, like a shift in consciousness is happening. This training day was an amazing experience for Sharon and me together. Amazing is the word I keep feeling, almost with tears of joy—it felt like amazing grace.

What is shifting here, Spirit?

Precious One,

"There is an awakening, a quickening in the soul of the people you touch and that touch you in this energy grid where you reside. This

is a precious time, though some of this will feel difficult for you to absorb fully, as the energy is big and your bodies will need to calibrate the new frequencies being attuned in your training. These frequencies will allow you to gather more information, to pick up psychic transmissions from other light workers, and to manifest new work in the near future for yourselves and others. What is really shifting is your capacity for love."

We leave the lights on for you!

Our new friend, Eddie, and his colleague Barbara, who partnered with him for psychic readings, were seated in front of me, crossed-legged on floor pillows. My long-time friend Marilyn, who wore the best honkin' jewelry I have ever seen in my lifetime, sat to my left. I had invited her to do a renewal session with us as she had been through the first class with me six years earlier. Sharon, sat to my right in her comfy clothes, her hair thin from the chemo and tucked under a colorful bandana, completed the small circle of Reiki students in the lobby of Health Ecology. Veronica stepped from her office wearing a long teaching robe of purple-and-lavender, quilted, silk patches, a departure from the typical white jacket, green scrubs and clogs she donned most days. She appeared six feet tall in the robe and was radiant.

Veronica introduced everyone and indicated that she would first tell us the story of Dr. Usui and how Reiki – the Universal Wisdom and life-force energy came to be 'rediscovered,' and then we would go through an attuning. She said it would not be until the second session that we'd begin our actual practice.

Settling in, she intoned, "The principles of Reiki mirror many eastern philosophies... that we must be present, be in our bodies and mindful of the work we do. Our monkey minds wander into our past and into our futures. The practice of claiming the principles—just for today—centers us, allowing us to heal in the space and time healing occurs – the present."

I watched Sharon, as Veronica continued to instruct us and answer questions from the group. Her face glowed with possibility and hope.

After hearing the story, we moved into the long hallway just outside the treatment rooms. Candles and incense invited us to take our places in a line-up of chairs that faced the same direction. We sat reverently as we listened to a tape of music and chants. Veronica worked behind us, over our heads, attuning us. It felt to me like we were small radio receivers and she was tuning us into the right frequency, or the radio waves running through us, giving us access to this signal, this gift of healing.

Sharon and I left the session in an altered state of consciousness. Neither of us spoke all the way home. I don't remember her getting into her red BMW to leave the house. Returning the next day, we began the practice of healing. We moved our hands into the pre-scribed positions, as if we were dancers, —first position, over the face, —second position, over the throat - and so on, until we had covered the entire body. Each of us had a turn on the table while our fellow students worked over our bodies. The energy around Sharon almost lifted her off the table. Once again, I felt the heat rush from my hands to my elbows when we began her session. As I looked up to find Veronica, I saw something else - a ball of swirling lights, almost like stars, behind Veronica. My mouth fell open, and I stared at the beautiful huge ball – it must have been three feet in diameter. Veronica saw me and explained, "Some of you may be seeing Dr. Usui. He shows up as a large ball of lights."

I was humbled at the sight. I bowed my head in acknowledgement without speaking. The ball of light moved up and down in response.

After this training session, Sharon and I practically glided out to my car. "Well, girlfriend, what's on your mind?" I inquired, as she slipped into the still new, tan leather, 'not-yet-orange-from-hands-full-of-goldfish-crackers', passenger seat.

"We are on a mission from God," Sharon said as we left the training, images of the Blues Brothers dancing in both of our heads from her impish interpretation. "I think I saw my angels when the attuning started yesterday. Today, while I was on the table, I know I saw them, moving in and out of my mind's eye as white light, morphing into beautiful faces. This is how I was supposed to live. This is what I was meant to do." She touched my right arm as she said, "Thank you for bringing to me to this place."

I thanked her for reminding me that this is at least in part what we were meant to be doing together in our work on this planet. We sat quietly together for a while in sacred silence.

We didn't hide this spiritual gift from others, yet we were mindful not to just throw ourselves open to unwanted teasing or questioning or to misuse the power we were tapping into. We were equally reverent and irreverent, laughing with each other about our power surges when we initiated the healing energy as a practice with each other, particularly as Sharon felt she needed it. At the same time we were hopeful, believing that this could, and would work to heal her.

I went to see Veronica on my own a few months later and she did a personal version of the second-degree class and attuning, teaching me to use energy from a distance. I learned to use the symbols passed on from Dr. Usui, and to heal from a country mile. Eddie and Barbara did the second-level initiation as well. Sharon and

I had regular sessions with them after the first radio encounter. During the session I was also told that much of my work with language would be designed to heal—my voice carried a vibration that would open the pathway for healing at many levels.

The baby had started moving a lot. Veronica told me that when I was attuned, so was he. He swam joyfully when we "turned on the heat."

Interpretation

Dear Diary,

I called Eddie Conner for a reading today and to interpret last night's dream, which terrified me and made me think I might have cancer, like Sharon:

"Dreamed last night about being in a beige-and-white area and having tall 'beings' draw fluids from my body, checking out my physical condition. I was being moved on the back of a golf cart from room to room. I was told that my levels were 17 and Sharon's were 25 and that it if I wasn't careful, I would have a 25 or higher level."

Eddie began, "There are light overtones, not heavy, in this dream. A large being of Light with a high vibration-frequency and a long, silver-mesh robe is holding a staff — the staff has magic crystals in it—pewter and gold in color. An energy field holds stones in place,—many of the stones are round/tigers eye, blues and whites, some amethysts. There is a message coming through from him:

"Golf cart — what is your relationship to golf?"

I responded, "Don't have a lot of time for it. I enjoy it, though."

"And, how do you play?" He asked.

"I am rather impatient," I replied. "I walk to the tee and hit the ball without a lot of aiming or practice."

"EXACTLY! Your relationship to time and patience is a big part of your dream, and they are the same thing, —"Time is Patience". What is your hurry? And what might be available to you if you aimed or practiced something you enjoyed playing?"

"I guess I would improve my score, enjoy playing more."

"Exactly. This dream feels like it is about getting into a new swing and being patient with yourself."

Eddie said, "Your guide wants to leave with this message, I am always with you, I am always just a thought away, in your mind's eye."

"Who is this guide?" I inquired.

"Leviathon. One of your many guides. A very powerful one. The one in the mesh robe."

"They have names like that?"

"Yes, they always have names. It is in the naming of things that Spirit brings them to life!"

Eddie said very little after the session that day. He just left me alone with the questions and my inquiry, searching for my own answers. The space between what we ask and the answer that is right for us, the space where two worlds—the world of spirit and the physical—touch, had become my new home.

Bowling

March 30th, 1993

Dear Diary,

Baby Hank! That's the name of the little boy we've invited to live with us. I saw him today through the ultrasound, swimming around in his liquid cocoon, already formed into a sweet face and full body — fingers and toes all there. We are naming him Hank for Barry's father, who died when Barry was 14.

I wish I could put into words how I feel about becoming a mother again. For one thing, I will be using an epidural this time. The hospital will hook me up when I get there. I am not doing the all-too-natural thing again and spending five days in the hospital waiting for my eyes to regain their focus. I mean, I love the notion of being "all natural and earth-mother-like," but giving birth is major medical and I have seen the major part of it, thank you very much. They don't call it "labor" for nothing. I do believe that motherhood is a sacred contract with God, and those who choose to become a mother are taking part in creation, the most powerful force. That said, I want to enjoy this experience and I trust that God gave us the intelligence to make drugs too!

I sat on the back porch today, a beautiful spring day, playing with Jess, and all I could think about was how this would be my last job in radio. I couldn't imagine working 70-hour weeks with two kids. When Barry came home and found us playing, I told him, "You know, I have no idea why I am saying this, other than I have this strong sense, this feeling—this is my last job in radio. I have no idea what's next for me, but I am ready for whatever life hands me." 'God Bumps' ran the length of my body after making that declaration.

Sharon is getting better. She has cut her hair really short to match the new growth, so she is still in wigs. Barry and I took her and Steve bowling on Saturday night. Because we thought we might bowl badly, we put our names on the lighted scoreboard as Fred, Wilma, Betty, and Barney—the names of our favorite cartoon characters, the Flintstones and Rubbles. Sharon slammed down a beer and ate greasy cheese pizza from the snack bar. As we posted our final score of the first game (with me, the Mommie Weeble scoring a whopping 107 as Wilma, and Sharon, as Betty, in at 148), Barry leaned over to me and commented, "You know how lucky she is? She wouldn't be here with us slamming down beers and rolling gutter balls if she had continued her therapy the way she started."

As we were leaving the bowling alley, we played a few arcade games. We won Venetian-blind sunglasses, and we all donned them on the way to the car. As we pulled out of the parking lot, Barry picked up the mobile phone and started singing along with Bruce Springsteen, "It takes a leap of faith to get things going—it takes a leap of faith—you got to show some trust."

What fun...What an amazing night. I swear I smelled Tube Rose snuff in the arcade.

Maw Maw — are you there? Did you ever go bowling?

"Once...and I was really bad. There were people setting up pins at the back of the alley, and I was terrified I would hit them. I didn't see the sport in it. I preferred fishing. I loved it when there was just me and the water and the fishes, and your grandpa yelling instructions at me about what I wasn't doing right. I actually enjoyed everything I did so I had a good time, but it wasn't my best thing. Cooking was!

Your friend Sharon is a gift. She is lighting the way. Your heart is also shining through in all that you do. You are my sunshine."

I Love You, Maw Maw

Playing made every challenge seem lighter during this time. It was easier for Sharon to stay focused on her healing when we just focused on playing. I considered the TV interviews I had seen with the Dalai Lama, who always seemed to laugh when he talked. When asked about it, he offered something to the effect, "the purpose of our lives is to be happy. When we fail to see the humor in life, the wisdom in lightness and compassion, we suffer." So we played and we laughed. We were way over the need to suffer.

I wondered if the power of our words – particularly words that come from a heart place and high-level frequency – could draw to us the experience of being happy, even when faced with the drama of losing our lives. If so, in the space of laughing aloud I questioned if we give ourselves more hope, if we learn to trust that "all is well," regardless. I know there is a time for laughter, a time for sorrow, a time for crying. This was a poignant Bible teaching that stayed with me. Yet, trusting the power of attraction I also trusted that our laughter gave us a sense of well-being. So we found reasons to laugh...at almost everything.

Birth

September 2nd, 1993

Dear Diary,

Yesterday, we welcomed our Baby Hank. I received an epidural, which was quickly followed by delivery an hour later at 2PM. Hank looked at me right after he was born, put his hands over his eyes as if he were blocking the light, and then looked at Barry. Then he was whisked away for drops in his eyes, weighing, finger-pricking, and all the other harsh stuff done to babies to welcome them to the planet. The hubbub was over in plenty of time for us all to watch the Phillies in the pennant race. Barry put a Phillies hat on Hank's little red head. From the look on Barry's face, this was a moment of total contentment, a feeling of exquisite happiness.

I brought a new-born baby doll to the hospital to share with Jess, but she just wanted to see Hank's "face and his other parts." I pulled the blanket back and showed her every perfect inch of her baby brother, the image of his father, except for the screaming red hair, which was more the color of my dad's.

He won't nurse, seems more inclined to want a steak and baked potato. We'll keep working at it, but the nurses keep sticking him in the heel trying to see about his blood sugar levels, and he has cried so hard that he's been throwing up bile. I have asked them to stop and they keep saying something about him needing to eat so they can get his blood sugar levels right.

I heard myself shout, "Then give him a bottle, for crying out loud, and stop sticking him with needles!" We ended up in the infant care nursery and out of the maternity birthing center, where a woman who spoke no English was screaming her baby into the world, while her husband repeatedly hit his head on the floor in the hallway outside my room praying loudly in Farsi. On most days, I would have thought this interesting or even lovely...but not today——I just wanted some peace.

I wanted to escape. I pushed myself up off the bed and walked down the hall to get my baby from the nursery. I intended to keep Hank in my room – wasn't going to let anyone else touch him. The nurse who had been sticking him every 15 minutes came in red-faced and obviously angry and I gathered my belonging as she placed me into a wheelchair. She rolled me, with Hank in my arms, as fast as she could into an elevator. She was either over-worked and pissed, or afraid of me. I couldn't tell, but I was happy to be going to a brighter floor, away from the machines, the screaming women, and the nurses with needles.

Barry had gone home for some sleep, and Marilyn had come to try to help me with the feeding. She was the midwife to mother-hood for me. She walked beside the chair, finally offering to take me to the next level for the children's hospital. I was at ease when she took over behind the wheelchair.

We were there a couple of days because Hank couldn't get the rhythm of eating. I swear if he could have talked, he would have said, "Cheeseburger and fries with some hot sauce and maybe a margarita." We finally got our act together enough for all the doctors and nutritionists to feel okay about our leaving, and we made our way home. The day after we got home, I had Hank on the diaper-changing table and he looked around the room—first at the primary-colored dots on the wallpaper, then at his name in a primary-colored puffy cloud, then at me, since I was singing and cooing. Then he did something I had never seen a one-week old little one do before. He smiled. It wasn't one of those scrunched "I've got gas" smiles, but an alert, "thanks for putting my name on the wall," smile.

Something else amazing happened that night. When I put him in the crib, he had light shoot from his fingers, and around his body was a halo of white light. It was a light show. It might have been static electricity had it happened just once or twice, but it happened a lot. Noticing his light, I started comparing the colors to those around Jessica. Hers was indigo much of the time. His was often white or indigo and gold. I rocked Hank until he fell asleep every night, and then I kept rocking and watching him until it was time to rock Jessica, a ritual I continued over the years until her feet dragged on the floor and she was too long for both of us to fit in the rocking chair.

I wondered how Sharon would feel, seeing Hank right after he was born. She didn't come to the hospital. I heard she'd had a couple of tough days. But I knew she would be around soon to share the joy of this baby boy, the baby born on the birthday of her soul–mate husband. She did come around the first week we were home and spent time holding him, rocking him, and singing to him. She found her way to Jessica and spent time coloring and playing with her, leaving the baby in my arms, as we talked and I caught up on her medical news, which was all seemingly good for the time being.

Sold!

September 7th, 1993

Dear Guides,

They have sold the stations. Again, I have the feeling that someone has sold "me" as well. I totally understand from a business perspective, but what?—I go away for five minutes to give birth and they sell the company!?

The only a hint that this was a possibility was when I got a call from Rick yesterday afternoon, saying he wanted to come see Baby Hank, and that he needed to see me as soon as possible. Without hesitating, I asked him, "Who did you sell the stations to?" He responded, "DJ, please don't ask me to do this over the phone."

I didn't have a vote in this. Do they even know how much to ask for a radio station? Of course they do—what am I thinking?

He is on his way over now. I've been pacing around the house with Hank on my shoulder, and Jessica riding around my feet on her Big Wheel tricycle. It feels like a million years ago that I accepted the job as General Manager. It also feels like yesterday. I love my job. I love the staff. Oh my goodness! What about Sharon?

What now?

"Precious One,

Are you seeking an answer, or asking the question just to ask the question?

"What next?" is always the question on our minds while we're in our earth-bound bodies. It is the ego mind question, the one that houses our fears and keeps us stuck in this anxious state, afraid that we'll lose something, end up with less than someone else, be humiliated. It is the death of the ego that the ego most fears. The reptilian brain, whose job is safety, confused that survival instinct by housing all fears, not just the sense of fear that something or someone might actually kill us. It is fear that drives this question.

You might recall that you ordered this intervention on your back porch so you could ultimately be with your children. Remember saying, "This will be my last job in radio?" You knew the time was near for the change. Yet, even knowing at some level does not give you comfort?

*This is a time of trust — it will be a faith walk for you. It does "take
a leap of faith to get new things going," and after there is movement,
it takes courage to live in faith. Just remember, 'All is well.'*

"It will be all right, have a good time!"

          You know who we are!

"No, I don't know who you are," was my impatient response.
I recall wanting to scream..."I don't know who you are! Show me
your faces! Show me something so I can trust you, talk about you
and explain this thing that is happening to me."

I've had to learn to trust. That day was the worst day since
Sharon told me she had cancer. Rick came over alone, walked in,
saw Hank, held him for a minute, and said hello to Barry and Jess.
Barry tried to take Hank from me, but I held on tight. Whatever
Rick said, he was going to have to say it to me with a baby on my
shoulder.

Thousands of questions had run through my mind before Rick
knocked on the front door. How could they not include me in this
decision? What if I had wanted to put together a group to buy the
stations? Was the company sold because I was on maternity leave?
We had turned the corner. We were profitable. Was it not enough?

A leveraged deal with another station had been made the day
before. The reason this came down so quickly was that the deal
between the oldies station and the other hot hits station had fallen
apart, so now the company out of the West Coast area was making an offer at a time the shareholders (all family) thought to be
a good time to sell and retire some of the family's holdings. I found

out later that the owner of the oldies station thought twice about selling to this group once he met them and pulled out of the deal. It didn't take me long to understand why. The newspaper sold the license, but no real property or tower, etc. The company had gotten a fair deal, he said, but when he told me what they had been paid, I almost threw up. They could have gotten three times that amount, given how these deals were being made at the time.

When he left, I handed the baby to Barry, kissed Jessica and went to my bathtub, where I lit some candles and meditated on important things, staying put until the water went cold. I cried for three days without stopping. My pillow was wet when I put my head down. Everything made me cry. Hank's crying made me cry. Jessica making Mommy pictures to make me feel better made me cry. Barry cooking for me, same thing. I lay in bed for much of the next day. Rick had sworn me to secrecy. I had to meet the new owners before I could tell anyone, or else the money deal to buy out my contract was off. I finally negotiated an arrangement to tell the engineer who had to take the new owners to the tower site as part of the closing, and McCall—I had to tell McCall. He had been with me for fifteen years and four moves. I couldn't imagine him being told in a room full of people. And then Sharon—could I at least tell her before the announcement was made public? They agreed to all of these requests.

I met the new owners two days later. I had to go to the stations at 5:30 AM and get all the files, take Jessica to the Montessori school, and then drive all the way to the attorney's office in Durham where we were scheduled to start the process of closing the deal by 7:00AM. Hank was in tow, as the nursing routine was still too tentative to stop and start. So, I arrived with a baby carrier, complete with new baby boy, two brief cases full of files, and a diaper bag thrown over my shoulder. Mr. New Boss was the first owner I met, a stout, round man in a fine, navy blue suit who tried to shake my hand but offered no help with any of the baggage. I could only smile – no free hand to shake. Tagging along behind him was a tall man, also in a navy, pin-striped suit. Along the way, they were distracted, into a conference room, where they were apparently closing another deal to buy stations in another market somewhere. I was a non-factor. They didn't even see me. Thankfully, Rick and Dave saw me through the glass wall in the conference room and came to my rescue. Swarthy and tall, Dave took my fair-skinned baby and cradled him while I made quick work of parking the contracts on the table for review. It felt surreal that I was in the midst of a closing, when I should have been on my back deck rocking my babies. The stark contrast of a baby in his finest baby-blue Feltman Brothers day-suit against the dark, pin-striped business suits created a visual paradox. It was as if someone had painted a picture of pure innocence against a serious and often-corrupt, "dark" business background, one that was now demanding a life decision of me - "Here you go lady—either be the Mommie of the sweet and innocent or the General Manager in the shark pool of leveraged marketing decisions. Choose!"

The new owners came back after a half hour giving each other high fives. "We have had a lot of strange things happen at a closing, but never had one yet with a baby," Mr. New Boss laughed nervously. He still didn't look at me directly, but talked around me. He asked his questions of the men in the room. They deferred to me. I was pissed. Dave was pissed. Baby Hank was pissed. Meal time. I made no excuses as I took Hank to the ladies room where I stayed for awhile, feeding, and cooing and rocking, and giving little attention to the full time lapse.

When I surfaced, the new owners were gone. They had gotten everything they needed and were in the other room closing yet another deal. They asked to have dinner with me that same night.

They wanted to go to the restaurant with "the barrels of apples." All I could think of was Cracker Barrel. My brain had fallen out. Why would guys who donned custom-tailored suits want to take me to Cracker Barrel? Were they looking for comfort food? Not have enough time on the interstate lately?

As it turned out, they were talking about the world class Angus Barn, the Raleigh area's signature landmark with the barrels of lucky apples in the corner store. Nice place. Great food. Legacy family owned.

The memory of this is still painful. I took it all too personally. Maybe I was too invested. I had unexpectedly fallen in love with my work, my company of colleagues, and my lifestyle. And now it was about to change. All of it!

I observed them throughout the dinner of fine steak and sea-food as they explained that they already had hired a General Manager for our station who was in town to manage the oldies station they had purchased earlier that summer. The new FCC rules allowed for multiple station ownership, two-to-four stations in the same market, and this was part of their company's game plan to purchase as many stations as they could in a market and then leverage resources by reducing management and sales to just one staff. They said I could have my job for six months or a package. I smiled, knowing that I had a severance contract with the news-papers that resided in the human resources department and not in the station contracts.

But my heart sank. First, I had no interest in working for these guys, but now it was becoming clearer that there had never been an intention to "want to meet me," other than as protocol to under-stand the team and move in as quickly as possible. The warmth meter didn't go above "cold and hard" I reasoned, so this dinner was just a confirmation of this being my last job in radio. I slipped in and out of total judgment about these guys and how wrong they were in their approach, which I am sure they read in my face, and frankly, I didn't care. They had the compassion of earth-worms, if that, as I assessed in my emotional, post-partum state. I learned later that they were judging me in return, as living up to the "Dragon Lady" sign on my door, noting how tough-minded I appeared to be. The idea of judgment being a boomerang was a constant lesson for me.

I thought at the time that I would just leave—be happy to move on, happy to spend more time with my babies and with Sharon. I was eager, yet tentative to see what life held for me in this journey beyond anything I had ever known.

BOOK IV
MYSTERIES

My view now about Mysteries of Faith

*"A mystic sees beyond the illusion of separateness into the intricate
web of life in which all things are expressions of the single Whole.
You can call this web God, the Tao, the Great Spirit, the Infinite
Mystery, Mother or Father, but it can be known only as love."*

-JOAN BORYSENKO, PH.D. – THE WAYS OF THE MYSTIC

A journey is a trip to somewhere; and in my case, it has been more
than accumulating frequent-flier miles on a big airline. I became
a traveler when I was ten, journeying within as I played with the
Ouija board, keeping a diary note that indicated I wanted to be an
airline stewardess instead of a T-E-A-C-H-E-R when I grew up.

I didn't think of myself as being a teacher until someone else
called me that. I also didn't think of myself as a mystic until one of

my gal pals told me she thought I should have written "Intuition for Dummies" and that I was the most mystical, magical human being she had ever met. Soon thereafter I mentioned her comment in jest to a couple of colleagues and one of them cautioned me, "Watch that word, DJ—you don't want to be considered a mystic. It will rock your world. People won't know what to do with you." That frightened me because I respected this man, mainly because, as is typical of southern women I often deferred to men I considered to be smarter, more educated, or more in tune with the world of business to tell me what I should or shouldn't say about my work.

In hindsight I realized I had internalized this voice of fear and limitation from an atheist, though he was a very wise and wonderful man, he believed in nothing greater. The more I ruminated over this warning, the more I noticed that all of my internal voices started fighting over the words and stories I would use in this book. They were all "winning," each at different times, so I became stuck and completed nothing other than wrestling with the title— Mystic Grits.

A big part of my exploration was into the word "mystic" which I discovered derived from many faiths and was ultimately a description of someone who had direct access to the Divine. In my world, that meant we were, and are, all modern mystics. In studying the archetype work of Dr. Carolyn Myss, I learned that a mystic can be defined as one "who follows a selfless path and practice to achieve union with the Divine, or lives in a state of enlightenment, with a shadow side of self-importance, being special or excluding others."[3] Including that anyone who believes in the Divine, in God, in the Tao, in the Great Spirit, regardless what we call Him or Her or It, made this new label and made me just normal enough.

We are living in a world of modern day mysticism. Every religious tradition, including Christianity, has had its version of mystics. Mysticism is defined on the world's open space dictionary, Wikipedia, as "the pursuit of, communion with, identity with, or conscious awareness of an ultimate reality, divinity, spiritual truth, or God through direct experience, intuition or insight." That's it. Nothing scary about that. This was essentially what I was taught as a child—simple steps such as, "pray each day—appreciate—say a blessing before you eat, realizing that your food comes from the great earth—express gratitude—forgive—find your passion in service—bless your connections—and observe the miracles in everyday occurrences." Nothing scary about these things either. Perhaps we are actually circling back to something that was true at some point in our past—something that was somehow banished out of misunderstanding.

Perhaps it also means that if you have a thought about someone and they call you within a few minutes, or if you sense a danger before it happens and get out of harm's way, or if you help someone by simply praying for them, or if you hold the space to listen and see new possibilities for others, you feel a connection with God. And if you connect directly with the Divine, just realize that you could be labeled a mystic – and remember there is really nothing scary about that.

Letting Go

September 17th, 1993

Announcement Day

Dear Guides,

The stations have been sold. I feel strange — a sense of freedom, yet a tremendous sense of loss. I am not sure whether to celebrate or to cry. So much emotion is stirring in me. I have no questions today, just wanted to tell you, that I will trust. I will TRUST— and to ask you to "show me the way."

> Your Pen Pal,
> Precious!

The announcement about the sale of the stations was made after what appeared to be an eternity of waiting.

Everyone was seated or standing around the conference table when I moved from my office into the conference room with the new owners early that September morning. Rick and Dave stood to my right and the new owners to my left. Rick made the announcement. All eyes shifted instantly to me to see my reaction. I felt only love for my team, the talented group of people I had come to know as my professional family and friends. I looked directly and calmly into each person's eyes as the announcement continued, resolute that we would all be okay.

Then it was my turn. I had not prepared a speech, and had no idea what I would say. This is what came out, as best I can recall.

"This company did not purchase the purple leather chairs and this beautiful new facility; they purchased the talent of this group – your talent, your leadership ability to perform beyond expectations. I have given birth to two babies, and in a way, I have given birth with you all to what exists here." I grabbed my still soft and swollen belly and added, "At least it feels like that," seizing a moment of irreverence and disarming the new owners.

"I have been told over the past two days that these guys will take great care of us, all of us. This team will become a part of a larger broadcast organization and, therefore, will have more resources to do the kinds of marketing we have always wanted to do. I have been told that this company has an investment in this community and are committed to foster relationships with our advertisers and listeners — that their goal is to have a seamless transition. As I sat and talked about all of you last night over dinner, I also realized just how much I love you—all of you—and how much I want to be with you. So that is my plan, to stay connected, to stay in this role for as long as it makes sense for me to do so. And I also told these guys that you would hold them to account for any promises they make, and I cited some examples of my own lessons about keeping promises with you."

I introduced the new owners by name and position. They said a few words about how they thought we would all like working for their company, but their words felt flat, empty, and fruitless. Most of the team looked at their feet. Sharon's face was white, her eyes sunken. She couldn't look at me. I am glad she didn't. I might not have made it through the speech at all.

I wanted to help make the transfer go well but it just wasn't in me yet. It wasn't in them yet, either. As the room emptied that morning after the announcement, I sat, emotionally spent, in my office. The conference room was taken over by the owners, who were working another deal with their attorney for a station combo purchase somewhere in the southeast.

I was witnessing an investment game feeding frenzy.

I stayed in the office for a while to have conversations with any of the staff who needed to talk through this. They asked the questions always asked of a leader in limbo: "Are you okay? What are you going to do now? You aren't leaving us are you? What else aren't they telling us?" Fearful expressions and anxieties arose, despite what I said.

I left the office to go home and rock babies. After all, I was still on maternity leave.

As I sat on the back porch rocking Hank, Jessica playing at my feet, I could feel my breathing. I noticed every inhale, every exhale. I closed my eyes and paid attention just to my breath—my life-giving breath. It had been a long while since I noticed the beauty of just breathing, letting go of what I held onto as a reality and breathing into a new way of being.

I would soon learn that "Letting-Go" and "Surrender" are two distinct experiences.

Surrender

So Diary,

Why is this transition so tough?

"To make a life change requires that you give up – surrender – to
something greater, something you cannot see. This may always be
a most difficult lesson. You have always been a generator, able to
make things happen in your own way, to make the best of things,
trusting they would turn out okay. You have been able to accept
whatever life hands you, trusting your own resilience. Now your
lesson is learning to trust, to really trust that these events are setting a new course in your life, one that is purposeful, one that has
a built-in guidance system to show you the way. You must truly
surrender now—literally allow this to be out of your hands, out of
your mind. And before you act, observe first—see what is happen-

ing. Your actions are now to simplify, follow your joy, moment-to-moment and stay true to that. Send us messages of appreciation for all that brings you joy. When it comes to the decisions you will face, speak only your own truth. All other words will taste like metal in your mouth now.

And remember —You ordered this Divine intervention!"

Your Guides from the Lighter Side!

I meditated again in my garden tub that night and I tried to release the emotional baggage of letting go, learning to quiet my mind and simply surrender to being present. I was breathing, "inhaling and exhaling," slowly, but this required something more of me. It required a release of boundaries, of things that had defined me. This felt like real work.

Wondering what was next, but not fearing it, I looked into the mirror the next morning and saw an angel. My face had literally morphed into a more-beautiful, translucent face, a version of me-only better. "Ah, this is what I keep trying to look like – this is what women are trying to achieve with all that make-up," I thought. Maybe we get a glimpse of our spiritual self in our dreams or when we are in a super-conscious state, and then we keep trying to find that underneath the warts and moles. This is what I want to see in the morning instead of dark circles under my eyes, large pores, chin hairs, and a bulb-like nose. This is the "me" I have always felt there underneath the surface appearance. "Wow....you go, girl. You go be beautiful!" I thought to myself.

The minute that thought crossed my mind, the story of Narcissus burned into my memory, and I was transformed back into my former self - the imperfect one, the one I tried to keep making better with Lancôme make-up and visits to my favorite spa.

When I went back to the stations two days later, I was greeted by the Chief Operating Officer, a new face. I almost ran to shake his hand. For some reason, I was excited beyond reason. His name was Mark, and he was equally curious about me, but he appeared to be an aloof cowboy, just as his colleagues had been in our first encounter. We discussed budgets, which I had prepared before Hank was born. I gave him what I had with an apology that it was not more-buttoned-down. I had also worked on my expected MBO (management-by-objectives) plan but didn't share that with him, as I wasn't sure if he knew the new company's strategy or plan for the stations. He said he would look over the documents and asked me if I wanted to take some of the managers to dinner that night with him. I agreed that was a good idea and we made arrangements.

We took about 10 people to dinner, just those who could change other plans to go with us. On the way to dinner, I dropped by the house to introduce Mark to my family. It was only then that the ice melted and he saw something behind the story he'd been told, and I saw in him a level of compassion that gave me a sense of connection. He looked at baby Hank for a long time, and then talked to Barry, who stated clearly his wish for Mark to take time to get to know me, to understand what I had built.

It was a pleasant-enough evening with Mark becoming visibly interested in each person. A thought crossed my mind as I sat next to him that night—"Oh, I have missed the point. These guys think I am disposable because I am on maternity leave. I have just had a baby, so it is a natural next step that I would simply want to leave now while there is a reason to go." And the minute this thought crossed my mind, Steve McCall looked at Mark and asked, "So what's going to happen with our boss?" Red-faced, Mark said, "We are not sure yet. This is going to be up to her." Others chimed in, and you would have thought I had been canonized. It might have gotten funny to me to see them so protective, had they not looked so serious and worried.

"It is going to be up to me?" I questioned to myself, knowing they planned to announce that the other manager would take control of both stations within the next day or so.

The next morning I met with Mark, and as he seated himself in my small corner office, he said, "So, are you trying to impress us?"

"With what? What do you mean?" I was confused.

"The budget planning. The loyal staff."

I pulled the current year's MBO plan and budget from the shelves behind my desk and, more-than-somewhat annoyed, dropped them on the granite table in front of him. "No sir. If I had wanted to impress you, I would have done one of these." Tears stung my eyes when I thought about the 'loyal staff,' and how to explain that.

He seemed stunned at my straight answer and reaction. I was about to fume, when he relaxed and said, "You know something? I think we may have been wrong about you. What do you want to do? Your team obviously wants you to stay."

"I thought you had this all determined," I started, but he interrupted.

"What if you stay for six months in your current position? What if we have two managers and then figure it out from there? Perhaps you can go to the home office out west to help us build some teams?"

Before I could think clearly, my ego stepped in and said, "Hot diggity dog! ... They want me to stay! They really like me!" Aloud,

I uttered a quiet question, "And what if the easiest answer is simply to leave?"

"Then why don't you talk to your team and see what they want you to do? The easiest answer may not be the right answer. You have invested a lot into this company, and maybe you want to see this through. This could be a great opportunity for you to be with a larger company. Consider giving us a try."

He left to make a few phone calls. Michael, one of the senior sales people, came in and said, "We are going to the airport to inquire about leasing a jet and making a trip to the new home office to see the big boys and let them know how important you are to us and our success. We really are, so stop us if you don't want to stay."

My stomach churned. Sharon came in, sporting her new wig. "OKAY, girlfriend, you know how I feel about you staying. Want us to hire a jet?" Sharon had started working full-time again just the day before. I longed to be in our daily conversations, but I had two babies at home. I thought I had made a decision already and that I was on a new path. I couldn't see straight. I couldn't speak, for fear of saying the wrong thing. The truth in that moment was "I didn't know what I wanted." I was completely confused.

Mark left with an understanding that I would think this through and get back to him... and also with my sincerest gratitude that he had made the offer. I had a phone meeting set the next day with the CEO. I called at our appointed time, as he had requested. He was not available. I called an hour later. He was still not available. I left a message with his secretary, "Please let him know I called for our phone conference at the time he scheduled, and that I need to leave to pick up children soon."

He called forty minutes later and shouted into the phone, "Are you hysterical? What are you trying to prove, getting me out of a meeting with State Athletics? We are signing the rights to carry their sports. Do you have any idea what it is like to be in a conversation to discuss 20 million dollars in revenue?"

I let him have it. "No, I am not hysterical. I am, however, somewhat upset. You asked me to call you at 3:00 PM my time today. I called and was told you were not available, and was told that you would get right back to me. I realize you are in a different time zone, so I thought perhaps I had the time wrong and I called again an hour later and was told you were in a meeting. And now you open a phone call by shouting about how important your other meeting is. And yes, as a matter of fact, I do know what it is like to be in a conversation for acquiring sports broadcasting rights with a university. I have been the sales manager for a network sports division of a broadcast company that was home to three universities and two professional sports organizations. If you'd been interested, you would have known that."

He stopped and said, "I have to go."

"You son-of-a-bitch," I thought. "You've made this an easy decision for me." I caught myself judging, and I didn't care. I had a really hard time forgiving what he "knew not," because he seemed to "know not much about working with women—or maybe even people in general!"

I called Rick right away. I told him every thought and word I said.

"Well that didn't go very well now, did it? This is not good," he responded.

Later that day, he called the CFO on the West Coast and two of the newspaper board members. He and Dave were on the warpath about how they perceived I was being treated and they wanted to mend my broken start with the new ownership. The sale of the stations had not been approved yet by the FCC; there was still time to quash the deal, so he felt they would be invested in making this transition smoother. I wrote a letter of apology to Mr. New Boss and held my breath.

I also called Star Capehart's cell phone. She was in a limo on the way to the Dallas airport. When I told her the stations had been sold and that I had a decision to make, she gasped, "Well that just sucks big-ole-greeeeeeennnn-donkey dicks!"

Guffaw.

I laughed louder and longer than I could ever remember, and snot flew out of my nose. I was embarrassed—I couldn't respond for laughing so hard. It was as if someone had released a pressure valve in my head. She ended the irreverent conversation as her driver approached the airport. "This is just the beginning, Doll Face. Don't you worry about a thing. This is a new beginning. But damn, it does change things."

I got a call the next morning from Mark, who was "on his way back within the week to sit down and talk," and he asked if I would hold any decision until he came to see me.

A building maintenance man with an elaborate tool belt also came into my office shortly after I hung up from the call. He said, "I got a message from someone here that you needed a recessed light changed." I looked up—all the lights were fine. "I am not aware of indicating I needed a light change," I challenged. "Well, best if I just check it now that I am here," he said flatly. I went to the conference room to get out of the way of the large fold-ing ladder, and I watched him climb up and poke around at one of the lights, unscrewing it and then screwing it back in. He didn't change the bulb. I watched him climb down, pack up, and step out of the office. "All set," he said.

Paranoia set in. No, it wasn't paranoia, it was total distrust. Had someone just bugged my office? I'd been warned by the owner of another station (who had decided against selling to them) that 'nothing was beneath these guys.' This was more than just a hunch. How the heck was I supposed to handle this?

The skin on my neck broke out in a rash. We were close to two months into this conversation now and I was dancing between a maternity leave and the transfer of ownership. If I chose to leave, the current employer would pay me a bonus, as I would be making a lifestyle decision. I prayed, "Just for today, I will be at peace." And then I continued, "just for today I will not judge these guys as assholes." I had a problem with accepting that I could actually not be in judgment, so I added, "They KNOW NOT, or maybe they are simply clueless."

I smiled at the fact that I was in total judgment and justified it as warranted, a means of discerning what I really wanted to do next.

The next morning I opened the trade publication, <u>Radio INK</u>. The article about our stations being sold was featured in the news column, and the new company was quoted as saying they "will be keeping both general managers."

The staff had reviewed the front-office copy, and as I walked out for my morning coffee, they cheered.

The lesson that seems to keep coming to me is this: If we don't consciously choose the thing that is for our highest good, the Universe and all of its resources will move us in a direction that at some level we intend to be moved. Perhaps surrendering was another way of learning to consciously choose a new path—and to acknowledge that a situation will move us to the next right thing, if we are willing to surrender to that truth.

Repeat: Tell the Truth & Surrender

November 10th, 1993

Dear Maw Maw,

You there?

I am in a huge conundrum. I have talked myself into staying with my team through the FCC approval of the license change and the transition of ownership. I am doing what I feel I need to do, what I believe to be the right thing. However, the maternity leave was way too short, given the circumstances.

Baby Hank now has his third respiratory infection in two months, for which he is being treated with serious antibiotics. Whenever possible, he's been in the Montessori School with Jessica, but we can't keep him out of the pediatrician's office. The infection seems worse every day, and he labors to breathe well.

Jessica was pushed off of a piece of playground equipment last week and broke her leg. The school's headmaster tried to have her walk, thinking that her leg didn't appear to be broken. When I arrived, I knew something was wrong when she kept asking for "stitches" (crutches) so she could walk better. We took her for an x-ray and found that she had indeed broken her left leg. She screamed as the doctor started to put the cast on her leg, and my blood pressure jumped so high I could feel blood pumping through my head.

Barry is being treated for walking pneumonia, and by the way, Mark and I were in the middle of budget discussions today for next year when Daddy called to inform me that Mom was diagnosed with breast cancer. It doesn't seem to be too aggressive, so she is going to wait until after Christmas for her surgery. He sounds really worried, though.

Maw Maw, tell me what to do now.

"Surrender. Just love those people in front of you each day, and surrender the rest."

You walk in love and light always,
Maw Maw

I held on until Thanksgiving weekend, when my baby boy was hospitalized with a heart rate of 172 beats per minute and was working too hard to breathe. His ribs showed through with every labored breath. I held him upright in a rocker for three days, as the doctors tried to determine what had caused the infection and how best to treat it. I sent healing energy through his body and prayed to God, Mother Mary, and all of his guides and angels to heal him. I sang, "Take me out to the ballgame," as they examined him and he would find my face and smile through the large plastic tubes making a mask on his face. A nurse walked in and tried to take him from me. I refused. She looked sympathetically at me as she said, "Honey, you are going to resent this baby if you don't get some rest." I had been rocking him for most of three days without sleep, and I had never felt anything but love and a belief that he was well at some level and would be showing signs of improvement soon. I whispered, "I appreciate your gesture, but I am not letting go. I hope you understand. And you must know that I could never resent this child. He is a gift with a purpose, so I will just wait here with him until he is better. All is well." She smiled and left after patting my arm.

Same journal date...

Angels, why do I see light around my babies?

"Welcome to the light show, Precious One. Remember how you saw the probe in the mountains many years ago? You have been opening your ability to "see" new dimensions. Your children have come to teach you this, among other things. Paying attention to the slightest awakening in them, simply observing their movements

and their questions will give you much to consider. Your children are light workers. They have incarnated at a time when the Earth desperately needs them, as have most of this generation's children. You can look into the faces of these old souls, into their eyes, and see wisdom that has not been here in such a mass of people before. They are masters, so you will need to learn to balance this appreciation of who they are with your need to teach them to live in a world that truly needs masters. This is why they chose you. They trust you, and they have a spiritual relationship and connection with you from the other dimensions of reality.

Enjoy the light show. Enjoy the children sent to you from heaven.

And, I will leave the lights on for you!"
Your Pal, Mikael

Hank got well enough to leave the hospital within the next two days. We both slept for almost 24 hours when we got home. My life was a complete blur. Jessie needed her Mommy, and I so wanted to be there for her too. She was beginning to have night terrors. I was feeling guilty about being away from her. She sported a new pink cast and wouldn't walk, so we took her everywhere in her Radio Flyer wagon with the wooden sides. Barry was still too ill to do much for anyone, though he tried valiantly.

I went to my garden tub and soaked every night for a week. I developed a routine of lighting candles and meditating. I was learning to meditate regularly as a way to stay centered and sane.

That night I asked this question, "What's the message I need to pay attention to now, given my family's health issues?" The answer was scribed in my journal.

> *"Your family has taken on your stress and has taken on responsibility for your decision. Heal yourself. Make your career decision—let go—and they will be well. Use the mantra, 'All is well' every time you encounter stressful circumstances. Choose everything you do, every thought you think, with love."*
>
> *Sonanda Christ*

I was at a precipice. It was time to choose a path.

When I arrived at work the first day after dealing with all of the family stresses, the general manager for the sister station had parked in my space. I felt violated. Not that it was really a big deal in the whole scheme of things; it was just confronting to find someone else parked in a spot that had been reserved for me for the past two years. When I walked into my office, I found him in my chair with his feet propped up on my desk. He sported gold designer sunglasses, which were pushed to the top his head. He had two, thick gold chains showing under his open-collared shirt, and several large gold rings were prominent on his fingers. He was playing with his key fob for the new Infinity that was parked in my space. That did it for me. This was the last straw – in arcade terms, "Game Over." I had really given it my best shot. When I had sensed that my office had been bugged, I decided to ignore it, and even had some fun with it. I just ran business as usual, as there really was nothing to hide in the way I was behaving. Besides, I didn't want to send a paranoid signal to the staff because I honestly wanted them to stay together and continue to build on the legacy we had started. That was the best thing that could happen for me personally, as well as for them, I reasoned. But this was different. I felt terribly violated with someone's feet on my desk. Instead of being able to lighten up and have fun with my new potential partner, which is more typical of radio characters, I felt victimized, and I don't do well in that state of being. I withdrew to the "fight or flight" space in my mind.

It was time to leave.

Mark flew in from Phoenix the next Tuesday night and I met him at the airport. I had made dinner reservations, partly because I understood that he had been on the road for a week and partly because I knew that my conversation couldn't wait until the next day. We had been talking by phone every week and had become fast friends. Underneath that corporate aloof façade was a cowboy with a heart. He was winning the staff over as well. We sat down to dinner at the European fusion restaurant, Parizades.

"I have to go, Mark. You know, the way this transition happened, it appears that you guys killed the Dragon Lady. You put her in a corner and took her power, and when rigor mortis sets in, she will surely start stinking up the place." I laughed. "You know what I am dealing with at home, and it's just time. I can still take my severance from the newspaper as a part of the sale of the station, and I'm willing to work a transition period with you to make sure everything is turned over in good shape. I have made my decision."

"This is what you really want?" he asked. I just nodded. We discussed how we would tell the staff after the holidays. I would remain on the payroll as manager and consultant for the next three months until the sale was finalized with the FCC. Relieved at last, we shifted the conversation and had a delightful dinner. I found a new kind of comfort food—feta cheese and lemon grass linguine with Bar-B-Que shrimp. I learned about his fiancé and her appreciation for the mystical. I heard a few stories of his childhood and how he came to work for this company and the owner. I learned more about how to appreciate what the president of the company was doing—and the fact that Mark had taken a stand for keeping me for awhile and how that had cost him personally with the owners. There was a softening in the dialogue and in our relationship. We determined that we'd be good friends.

I was finally able to sleep through the night, at peace with my decision, ready to focus on my mental, emotional, spiritual, and physical well-being, because apparently my family needed me to really, really give up and heal myself so they could all get well.

Predestined

December 27th, 1993

Maw Maw,

What is there to learn from a guided meditation? What can I trust about the guided readings and sessions with my new friend Eddie? This one has stayed with me, so I need to write it as I experienced it.

Sharon and I took a break from our crazy schedules today and went to see Eddie and Barbara for readings to start the New Year. I'm not telling everyone at the station about my leaving until after we return from the holiday and the entire staff can become a part of the plans for the transition. I promised Mark.

Eddie and Barbara took us into a guided meditation during the session, with Sharon and me lying side-by-side, on top of my bed with our eyes closed. They played music and took us into a deep, relaxed state. In my imagination, I envisioned a small version of me, a little fairy-like spirit doing spring dives out of my solar plexus, and then we were off into a story.

Sharon and I were a part of the same story, an unfolding of a past life together. We were in the West, immediately after the Civil War. Mark was there, looking the same as now, but he was wearing a military uniform. I was a young native woman, with a face similar to mine now, but with long, flowing, silky-black hair. I walked toward him, along with my younger sister, whom he seemed to fancy. She was beautiful. She was also someone I recognized — one of our current sales people. He ushered us all into the horse barn when other soldiers came through the town. He seemed protective.

There was another scene in which it was clear that we (Mark and I) had a child together, something I had hidden from him. I saw him from a distance when I was in the town picking up supplies. I was with child, but the elders had seen an ill fate, so I was warned not to go near him again. He had noticed me, but couldn't call attention to us by acknowledging our connection. In a later scene, I had a papoose and my younger sister was caring for the baby. I was an elder, smoking a pipe with the others in a tepee, and we saw visions of danger. We came out and instructed everyone to pack all their belongings and prepare to leave. I worked in the dirt, packing up my things and gathering my child with my sister. I handed the baby boy to her and started preparing her and my mother for a long ride on horseback. As I looked at my mother, I recognized Sharon with long, flowing, wild, white hair, and kind, yet sad, eyes. She was my mother and she knew. The rest of the village left slowly on foot or horseback, not looking back. Everyone left except for a handful of our finest warriors and a few of our elders. I stayed behind as translator, and to help tend the fires of the camp, something we had learned to do so the others could make their way into the hills to safety. Our intention was conversation, but we knew—we always knew about the fights with the white man. The others had a three-day head start. Through my dreams in my own tepee, I could see my son and my sister in the hills. I could also see the militia in town mounting for a fight. Those in charge looked very much like the new bosses I had met in the new company. In the next scene that I remember, I was lying on the ground, bleeding out, as Mark found me. He looked into my eyes and he knew. I confirmed, 'we have a son,' as I saw my spirit dance into the heavens. He stood up and screamed, tearing his clothing. It was the end of the unfolding scene, of my story from another place and time.

Eddie brought us back into a conscious state through a breathing exercise. I don't remember what Sharon said during the time we were "out," but the vivid imagery took me only a second to recall. They had scribed the scenes I had expressed as they prompted me with questions.

The interpretation followed:

"Well, our dear friend," Eddie started, "You have more than a metaphor for what you are experiencing now. You have a reason - -maybe even a karmic reason—to have drawn these people into your life. These cowboys, as you call them, have been around before, and it is not the first time they have taken your life or made you feel that way. This is the reason you knew them and reacted so strongly when you first saw them. They haven't evolved too much since this story was lived. Well, Mark has, but the others, not as much. He finds you fascinating because of how people follow you. He actually feels this karmic connection with you and may confuse that for loving you. He sees you with Baby Hank and can't sleep at night, but he doesn't understand why. He simply knows that he wants to protect you, and he is longing for a child of his own.

I found all of this confusing. I didn't want to see Mark in that light — I was sure my affinity toward him was based more on our seeing eye-to-eye and on the kindness he had shown. But I was postpartum for crying out loud — and wasn't feeling physically attractive — and hadn't considered a karmic type of connection.

To break my thoughts, I touched Sharon softly on the arm, and half-kidding, asked her, "So Mom, what was it like to raise me as your daughter?" I expected her to say something fresh, but she responded soulfully, "You were the one that the tribe heard. You were the one who held our voice and a vision, our ancestral story. I was the wise woman in this tribe, the one people looked to in many ways, but I had given birth to you and two others who were the seekers of knowledge, and you all had many gifts of the spirit. I showed you the ways of the people, but you were reaching beyond that. It was in giving birth to you that I was given the name of the wise woman, an Indian name that sounded to me like Gay-Ah—Yah."

"Gay Ah-Yah" Eddie confirmed, "or perhaps, Gaia – Earth Mother," I thought.

"And DJ, you need to know that McCall was your brother and that your son was Michael, our star sales rep," she finished. We were quiet for about 20 seconds, mulling this over. Then as if on cue, we both laughed out loud. Of course they were. How else should this story take shape but to include everyone we had worked with and known now, in another lifetime? I mean, if we were just drifting along and happened to land here in this space and time, then how the heck would everyone else who experienced life in a tepee with us not come back at the same time?

When the sessions ended, I wanted to run screaming out of my bedroom and hug my babies and never go back to the stations again. I wanted the safety of what I knew and loved to stay the same. I wondered if I could ever look at Mark the same way again. I mean, maybe this was just a story that came to me in this meditation, meant only to be helpful for my understanding. Surely this didn't really happen with all the characters from the radio station? I mean what are the cosmic odds of that?

Eddie turned to Sharon to say, "And, Sharon, you seem to be carrying forward a part of this story in this lifetime. Your purpose to bring these people together in this lifetime seems to be a big part of your story."

Eddie never says anything about Sharon having cancer. He holds her in a state of total health.

As I sit writing this, there is a strong smell of tobacco —

Maw Maw, Do you want to tell me something?

"In your meditations you are conveyed into a new dimension of spirit. You will find healing and guidance come in many forms here. Trust your heart, and you will know what is real, or true, and what is illusion. Just be mindful that what is real for you may not be experienced in the same way by others. There is no right or wrong way, or even one way—just the way life unfolds that you must learn to pay attention to. Remember, this is all an experiment, an Earth school for spiritual growth through a human experience. The precious gift of living on Earth is the opportunity to co-create with God out of your intentions and your declarations, your beautiful spoken language.

Karma is the eastern word that describes the essence of the Golden Rule, "Do unto others what you would have done unto you." It is found in every religion, including in the teachings of the Bible.

Karma simply means "cause and effect." You must learn that what you carry in your heart, as well as in your past, you will face in your future. The concept of Karma is taught so that people will become mindful of what they hold in their hearts."

Hold the truth of who you are in your own heart.

Love and Light,
Maw Maw

There was freedom in knowing that my time in the station was short, and I was plotting a new course. Sharon and I spent time philosophizing. I told Sharon and others about Maw Maw's answers to my questions. We ruminated over the possibilities. Most days there were belly laughs as we thought how "far out" our conversations had become. We laughed about how much there was that we didn't know, couldn't really know for sure. We settled on just asking better questions. We questioned our ideals, and we questioned how we exercise our faith.

Barry and I were involved in helping to build a new Methodist Church, and I was content in attending a place where I knew I could explore the mysteries beyond the basic tenets of the church that I had held dear as a child. I had to exercise my faith in a traditional way, because I needed a source outside of me to help guide me on this inner journey. I also needed the foundation of faith I had known as a child. I needed a place that grounded me and would allow me to build community. I needed a place to go on Sundays and see light around people. I needed a church home.

As I considered the "guided meditation experience" in the quiet time in church that next Sunday, I held that anything was possible. Maybe I was in love with a slow walking cowboy soldier once. Maybe I was on another planet once. The truth is that "there is very little I can know for sure."

I looked up from my thoughts and noticed light around everyone standing in front of me. The entire congregation was shrouded in a white light. When Pastor Rick moved, he left a light trail behind him. When I noticed it, it grew larger and more intense, and I felt transfixed, as if I could see nothing other than this beautiful and very real light.

I went to the stations daily to check in, reviewing marketing plans, and discussing rate cards and ratings growth. But mostly, I went to the stations to have my awakening conversation with my dear friend Sharon and our colleagues. Sharon's hair was growing back to the lovely, normal, sun-kissed, ash–brown color I had seen when I first met her. She stopped wearing the wigs, and I began to see light around her head again.

Every day this spirit-filled dialogue continued around the computers, even as people wrote proposals for clients, or as people gathered in the conference room and seated themselves in the big, purple, leather chairs for tea. We read <u>The Celestine Prophecy</u> [4] and talked about our control dramas developed within -the intimidator, the poor me, the aloof, and the interrogator. The author, James Redfield, wrote that these are dramas 'we each have to some degree but that one is dominant in each of us, and we can see how they play out in our lives when we feel a need to control,' or when we are holding on to some fear. Sharon and I laughed about how I had mastered 'The Interrogator.'

Many of my colleagues were finding their own spiritual growth spurts. We had tapped into a new way of being together at work and were engaged in daily conversations unlike any that we had experienced at work before. It wasn't proselytizing. We were becoming more. And there was no ignoring it. It was simply being called forth from us in the sacred space created out of our soulful conversations to make sense of the challenges and changes we were all facing.

The result of this newly forming dynamic was that the everyday work of selling advertising and creating winning programming got handled effortlessly. We had set an extreme goal of doubling the revenue projections, and going for twice as much as the company expected. We kept two daily revenue update sheets, one with the real budget and one with our secret performance goals. We started hitting—and exceeding—the secret goals, growing at 40% in a market that grew at 7%. It occurred to me that I had better take note of this phenomenon. Maybe we had restructured something molecular, something we could never undo. We were being connected heart-to-heart for life, wherever our individual lives might lead us. This was an extraordinary time. It felt magical.

Angel Names

"The important thing is not to stop questioning. Curiosity has its
own reasons for existing. One cannot help but be in awe when he
contemplates the mysteries of eternity, of life, of the marvelous
structure of reality. It is enough if one tries merely to comprehend
a little of this mystery every day. Never lose a holy curiosity."

−ALBERT EINSTEIN

I frequently drove Sharon to Black Mountain to the Energy
Medicine Clinic so she could try some alternative healing meth-
ods. Barry was sweet enough to watch the babies for me on these
occasions so I could have a few days away just with Sharon. One
special trip gave us time together that was particularly intriguing.

I had been reading <u>The Star Borne</u>, by Solara [5], while I waited for Sharon to complete her energy treatments one glorious summer day. I decided to attempt an exercise in the book that was designed to help the reader determine their angel name. I gave the book to Sharon to read when we got back to the Way Back Retreat, the place we stayed for her to recharge on these trips. We worked together that day before we made dinner, each of us writing away to answer the questions in the exercise, which was simply to ask for and meditate on our spirit name, our angel name. This next entry is what came to me.

"Greetings to you Narastar

—this is your angel name!"

Thank you for acknowledging me. I am your guardian and guide — your spiritual pen pal. You are now entering a time of swift change and accelerated growth. You will tend to make this time difficult. Relax into the unknown. Let it come to you as it always has. We will bring you to the next source of your Earth's work. It will be in the entertainment and educational field, in the communication form of teaching. You will complete your book(s). The resources you seek—financial, personnel, time — are all transmuting and crystallizing. In a wink, you will be a bearer of our story, The Angel Story, and you will give credence with your story because of who you are and what you have done to date. Much of what you will do is to channel the information from the angel kingdom. If you choose to write about Fear in the workplace, you can do that, but most of what you will be doing is to convey information from the other side, from me."

The name Narastar is powerful in the angel kingdom and belongs to a soul group of thirteen different spirits. Thirteen is the transcendent number, and you have all incarnated in this time of Earth's shifts to help the planet through its transformation.

"I am Michael, or Mikael, Archangel, Bringer of Light, and your personal guide."

"Uh, Sharon," I yelled in a matter of fact voice through our cabin at the Way Back Retreat. "I have been given an angel name and some information from the Archangel Mikael, although it appears I have been misspelling his name pretty much all of my life." I was more than half joking about what had fallen out of my hand onto paper.

She came around the corner from her bedroom where she had been writing. With goose bumps visible to the naked eye and eyes as big as saucers, she explained, "I just got my angel name too. It's Solara, which they said means 'Of the Light.'"

"Geez Louise!" I thought. The mountain air must have been making us lightheaded. We both stood still, ten feet apart and stared at each other for a long time. Then she picked up her journal to read to me. I recorded her message from that day too. Hers was a simple paragraph, although she had waited for what seemed an eternity to scribe it.

"You must learn to unlearn what you were taught about life as a child. You must learn to let go of what you thought was you in order to let the real you emerge. People fear the unknown, even within themselves. It is simply a part of you that you don't know or love."

Sonanda Christ, (as S.C.)

Sharon always collapsed it as simply "SC" to remind herself that these were also her initials.

We were unusually quiet on the four-hour drive home. I was certain that the information we had been given resonated with me. Yet, we both felt a huge responsibility. This type of information required a different type of "container." I needed to sort for a while.

Our circle of friends became an unstructured support group for Sharon during the days that followed. Sharon named me the general of the group, explaining that she had always known me as the General Manager of something and right now, it might as well be her health. She teased, "You could always become General Manager of the Universe—and you might pull it off, if you don't get in touch with your more feminine energies."

Belly laugh!

That statement, while made in jest, sparked an awareness in me that I needed to make a necessary change in my life. I had operated for much of my career by being in touch with my masculine energy, consistently staying in motion – always acting. And, truth be told, that had served me well. Now it was time to succumb to the lighter, more feminine, creative energy, and patiently wait for my life to unfold, acknowledging a higher purpose or calling. I was learning that both energies served me well, I needed to balance them, relying more on the female or spiritual energy to guide my male energy into action.

I gave up any idea that I might have had that I could go back to the careers that once held me captive, and that had paid me handsomely. My work now was to become a guide of some kind, a way shower. But for what purpose? How? Where to begin? My wise friend and teacher held a key, of course.

I had never been in a relationship with a girlfriend who challenged me or loved me quite the same way Sharon did.

She challenged me because she was living a beautiful, courageous life, despite having a horrible disease. Watching her live in total appreciation every day, I learned to at least mimic that courage much of the time, trying it out to see how it felt to be fully present as I faced my simple fears of unknown income, while she faced the loss of her beautiful life. We were always focused on creating the future together, and I was learning that the future we all seem to concern ourselves with is created here and now – breath to breath. We live into tomorrow by the choices we make, moment to moment.

Completion

January 28th, 1994

Dear Maw Maw,

Today is Friday, my announcement day. I am leaving the wild world of radio. I feel a sense of freedom, but also a sense of tremendous sadness, like some part of me has died. I just wanted to check in and make sure you will be with me.

Dear One,

*"I am always with you. When you smell the tobacco today, know that
this is my signal for you to trust you are on the right path, and that
your heart is connecting with all those whom you are serving with
your words and presence. You are a leader of leaders. The others
watch you closely to see what is possible. You will see their lives take
on fuller meaning in the coming years as they go out from this place
to serve in new and more important ways. You have taught them
well."*

Love you so...
Maw Maw

I wore a black tunic and a Byzantine cross, my signal of the
departure from the traditional suits as I began my swan song that
day. Barry told me, "Go be strong .... Be at peace." Mark sat at the
other end of the table, and instead of being seated in my usual chair
at the head of the table, I perched on top of the table and crossed
my legs under me. I pulled out a copy of <u>The Celestine Prophecy</u>, we
had been passing around the station as fodder for our latest spiritual conversations which were thankfully still alive.

I opened the book and started reading about the "the Ninth
Insight" the way any drama queen who was doing a swan song
might read from such a book. I built on the conversations we were
all having about changing cultures and civilizations, about becoming more consciously aware of our individual contributions and
our purpose on the planet.

"Guided by their intuitions, everyone will know precisely
what to do, and when to do it, and this will fit harmoniously
with the actions of others."

"Our sense of purpose will be satisfied by the thrill of our own evolution – by the elation of receiving intuitions and then watching closely as our destinies unfold. The (Ninth) Insight depicts a human world where everyone has slowed down and become more alert, ever vigilant for the next meaningful encounter that comes along." [4]

Then I addressed my friends and colleagues more personally, saying something to the effect, "A short while ago, I sat on my back deck and declared this would be my last job in radio. I couldn't imagine being in a better place or having a more wonderful experience in this business. I am overwhelmingly grateful for all that I have experienced here and all the love I feel when I am with you all.

I didn't have a choice about selling these stations to a new company. The truth is I created this personal change with my declaration that day on my deck. Let this be a reminder of the power in old wives tales, "Be careful what you ask for!"

They all laughed.

I am obviously leaving the stations, but I will be around for the next few months, as needed, to help with the details of the transition. After that I am going to focus on being a good mommy for a while. I have no other plans, except to write a book someday soon about dealing with changes, a book I am now calling, "Facing the Dragon: Managing Fear in the Workplace."

The emotion began filling my voice, so Mark took over and finished the explanation of how we would be working together and what he personally wanted for my family. There was only love being communicated, and the staff was settled that this was the next best thing for me, and obviously the next best thing for them. They trusted Mark.

This was how a transition should feel. This is honest and forth-right. This is powerful.

I left the stations after the morning meeting and picked up Jessica from the Montessori School early. She was still in the hot-pink leg cast, sitting and waiting for me in the Radio Flyer wagon that we left at the school for the teachers to pull her around in. We went to get our nails polished. On the way home I told her I was going to become a stay-home mommy soon. She grinned from ear to ear. I looked at my nails at a stoplight and laughed, "Yep, no more Dragon Lady nails." She waited for a few minutes, and looked at me, her sweet voice dripping with excitement as she said, "No more dragon lady.... Now you are the mommy person!"

I hugged her tight. Now I am the mommy person. This was so right.

"*The Greatest Gift you can give others is the example of your own life work-ing,*" is a quote from Sanaya Roman written on a note from Sharon. It resonated with me and I wrote it down. My own life was begin-ning to work. I had money in the bank, time off with my kids, and possibilities to do things I had previously only dreamed of doing.

The week after my announcement, Radio Ink printed the news that I was leaving the industry, heading off to write a book. That was fourteen years ago. My word!—Has it been that long since I set out to do this?

I reached for another pile of journals I had covered in cloth and wrapped in plastic dust covers before placing them in the big box. Jessica yelled, "What's for dinner, Mom?" I took a moment to explain to her that it would be a good night for pizza. My legs were numb from being in the same lotus position for hours, and I was curious about what else is waiting to come to life from these forgotten pages.

Listening to Trees

March 1994

Dear Diary,

Sharon and Steve moved into their new treehouse in the
Red Bud subdivision out near Pittsboro... 10 acres on
the Haw River, forever away in the wooded countryside.
The land is magical there — beautiful hardwoods and
Carolina pines all around, and you can hear the fast,
deep river babbling nature songs at night. I went out today
for some journaling time with Sharon. She had a doctor's
visit yesterday, and they are encouraged by her progress.
She seems to be healing, and they are all hopeful.

Sharon's journal message was an introduction to one of her guides named Andrew. He was there to aid her healing and wanted to "Re-Mind" her that healing occurs at many levels. Sometimes healing is for our spirit self, sometimes for our physical self, sometimes for our emotional well-being, and sometimes for a past life—one that carried something over to this lifetime.

One of the most important associations for Sharon in this healing process is a developing communion with trees. She received guidance today to walk among them, to pick up their fallen branches and adopt a walking stick, to talk to them, to breathe in their power and return her breath to them, and, on occasions, to hug them!

As she penned her last sentence, she giggled and then read aloud, "And from the old wise oak tree, a message, "Tell Steve I said thanks for the earrings." We looked up at the two arty, copper bird feeders hanging in perfect symmetry from lower branches on the largest oak tree on the property's perimeter. They shimmered and dangled like earrings.

Belly laughs.

Sharon was getting stronger. We started a series of yummy potluck dinners, held each weekend at her peaceful place in the woods by the river. Many of our friends and radio colleagues came together to share whole foods and to try new recipes. Sharon was beginning to get creative with her own recipes, and she taught cooking classes to some of the neighbors and friends, though she still worked at the radio station. She had learned to make vegetarian sushi with cucumber, carrots, and avocado rolled in rice, seaweed sheets and toasted sesame seeds. This was one of my favorites, served with wasabi and fresh ginger. We prayed over the food as we prepared it, and blessed it before we ate it. After a couple of months of these gatherings, Barry finally asked me when we might get back to some real food at home and away from the macrobiotic style of cooking. "I'm not complaining," he said, "but some of this stuff tastes like cardboard."

The time we spent at Steve and Sharon's was always special. Jessica played with the petite canine family—Maggie a mutt, and Milo, a Yorkie Terrier—and we listened to Steve's old rock-and-roll LPs, while I toted Baby Hank everywhere, strapped in a baby carrier next to my heart. Although he was still working too hard to breathe, he was slowly healing as a result of our energy work. We had also taken him to a chiropractor, who muscle-tested him for allergens, so we knew not to give him cow's milk and to keep him from environments with commercial aldehydes, or smoke. Often, we were just quiet together, making kid jewelry with Play-Dough on the big deck, and soaking in the beauty of the woods, the river, and the deer that watched us come and go.

Meeting the Angels & Guides

February 2nd, 1994

Dear Diary,

In today's session with Eddie and Barbara, I had many questions. I wanted to:

- Meet my guides

- Talk about my book

- Understand what I will communicate in my work

- Discover more about building a pyramid

Eddie said, "Your guides are here and introductions will be made." (Barbara wrote their names here as they appeared.) Serving as intermediary, Eddie introduced me to my guides.

"Leviathon— he will help you with the Pyramid Project. You will be visiting countries—Great Britain, Spain, Japan—where he will make connections pre-arranged for you. He visits you on the astral plane.

Mikael — he will help you with relaxation techniques. His message is: Learn to "Be." Stop your "doing-ness," and you will be lighter. Meditate with candles.

Christ (Jesus, Sonanda, Joshua) — He asks you simply to "Trust" and to continue to love people. He likes that you honor him in your home. He will come to you in lights. Light candles and invoke his spirit. Sit with him and receive his messages of love.

Mary — She offers you the protection of the feminine. She advises you to stop thinking so much. You will see her in waves of light. She will help with the book from a feminine point of view. She also requests that you watch the children's diets. They are star children.

"Precious — Your grandmother is here. She is your deep soul connection to this plane of existence. All you will need to do to invite her to help with your work is to think her name, and she will be in your foremost thinking, in your mind's eye.

Your book will help people understand that there is only "love and fear" only two ways of being in the world. Your story of conquering fear — and achieving through love - will help people open the door to how they can overcome their own "fear." Fear is a lack of love, faith, and trust.

Your business will use the pyramid symbol; in fact, you will manifest the pyramid at many levels, including a physical building designed to anchor the power of healing and consciousness on the planet.

Write a list of all that you appreciate. Make it grand — include hundreds of things you love and that are working in your life. This will allow you to more easily attract the resources you need. Know that you are loved.

For now, just love the people we send your way.

Meeting the guides was a moment to remember. Their energy was so intense when they entered the space created by Eddie and Barbara, and they all started talking at the same time, as if they had been waiting for an eternity to say hello. As I started to say something about hearing many voices at the same time, Eddie stepped in and made a request, "You are all beautiful and quite excited, but could you please introduce yourselves one at a time, so this Precious spirit can hear this information?"

After a moment of silence, they did. They came to me gently, playfully, yet respectfully, one at a time. I could sense them, even when I couldn't see their faces. I had images of them. They smiled at me, and I saw them, not as pictures I had seen before, but as real people dressed in period costumes to place them here in a specific time. They looked deep into my eyes, and I recognized each as an aspect of myself, as if I had been morphed from the energies of all of these amazing spirits, or people.

Frustration

March 23rd, 1994

Dear Diary,

Maw Maw, angels, guides —

I am so frustrated. I have this sense of starting and stopping this business endeavor over and over. What is there to know about being "upset?"

"Ah Precious One —

The upset that you and all others experience is that you always feel you need to do something other than what you intend to do. Jessica now has the measles, and Hank still is fighting respiratory infections. You feel that your children are ill much of the time. Sharon's illness, your mother's recent cancer surgery, and your children's health concerns ask more of you. They all demand your concentration.

It is time to pursue alternative paths for your children's health care. They have lived on antibiotics to heal their viral infections, which is the wrong antidote. It is time to focus on their complete well being. Your intention to do that will also serve you.

You are also mourning the loss of your "self" in other ways. You are weary of having others offer sympathy about leaving your position with the stations. It is time to go within, to simply be with your family.

A lot of love goes into the food you make for Sharon and your family, and a lot of love comes from the meals of your childhood. Send that love into all the food you make. And remember, being a caretaker, a healer, is honorable. Unless you go through these challenges in those roles, how can you have compassion for others who experience them? How could you learn to teach others what they will need to know to manage their lives in a divine way?

This is part of your shamanic journey. Relax into the flow of your life. All is well.

It was true. I had an enormous capacity for work, and I loved it. I loved the feeling of creating and producing something. I loved the motion in business and the joy of watching myself and others gain some new insights or awareness. So, the idea of settling into simply being present with my children and my friends and not worrying about building anything was welcome, but the lack of activity was foreign to me. I had only a vague notion of what it meant to "relax into the flow."

Atlantis

April 11th, 1994

Dear Diary,

Sharon and I had readings today with Barbara and Eddie. Actually, mine was a guided meditation to Atlantis, the lost civilization.

At one point, my inner spirit, that fairy-size version of me, sprang out of my solar plexus and into the rhythm of Eddie's words, as I found myself breathing out to release the day and enter into meditation. With my eyes closed, I saw two cylinders of white light, tremendous columns of moving, hot energy, to my left, and a crystal pyramid in front of me. The people of Atlantis, thousands of them, were moving toward us, their faces filled with terror. There were stairs of light to our right. People were ascending the stairs, changing their frequencies, and becoming light as they began leaving that dimension. Our purpose was to help them transform and move to another plane, another space and time — and perhaps to another planet. That's how it felt. We were not afraid. Barry was with me, always to my right. He wore a crown of some sort.

After everyone else had left and Atlantis was evacuated, the thirteen of us raised our hands above our heads, finger tips together, (as if we were going to pray). A powerful beam of light formed, extending from our outstretched hands into the heavens, and we ascended the beam of light until we changed frequency and became light also.

Barry and I fused into one light, flame red in the center — white light with green around it. Twin flames.

Then Eddie and Barbara took me back 20 years prior to that experience. I was working in a temple located at the base of a mountain. The temple roof was supported only by white, marble, columns, providing an open view in all directions. This sacred place was the entry, or foyer, to subterranean crystal caverns and chambers. I wore an artistic crown with a large ruby stone in the center. It was made of shimmering gold and silver metals, but it also held white, iridescent, crystal and crushed, pink and turquoise stones in the top of it. I sensed it had its own power. All the temple workers wore the same color. Hank was there, appearing to be a knight of some sort, and Jessie was dressed as a temple goddess, older than me. I was very feminine, very powerful, a healer. I touched people's foreheads and opened their spirits for healing.

This was Atlantis. It felt as if we were on another planet — not necessarily Earth. It seemed to be a garden where we diverted/reinserted energy through the use of crystals in these cylinders or columns of light. Over time, the energy that we worked with shifted, as a result of the misuse of power. We ended up destroying the place during our "experiment." In the end, I watched the energy cylinders crumble into the sea.

During this meditation my hands felt huge, as if they were three feet long! When I came back to a conscious state, I felt energized. Although my hands were still quite warm and felt larger than normal, my body was cold, and I was shaking.

Up until that day, I had known about Atlantis only through stories or songs I had heard. Visiting it was confronting. Among the communications I had given to Eddie, who scribed the details of this journey, was this note on twin flames: Originally one flame – separated, like a cell is divided, to balance energies. Each side must marry its own masculine and feminine energies here on earth. Twin flames have always been mirror reflections of each other – since the beginning of our time.

"Greetings, Angels,

Since you have sought our instruction, we will remind you both of things you already know:

On "Atlantis" you're getting warmer. Atlantis was a civilization of beginnings and human creations. In universal terms, it was a very young civilization when the energies shifted. You both lived for almost the entire span of human civilization.

Many of the lessons there are also lessons here. There was a caste system, because there were souls in evolution then, just as now. Not every human was supposed to teach, or where would you find the need for students? Not every "low" citizen was "lowly." Many angels incarnated into suffering to teach evolving masters how to open their hearts, how to love.

Some of you who raised your frequencies became ascended masters in the end. You worked with the energy fields grounded by humans. Most people misused power because there was so much readily available. That's why you have agreed in this incarnation of experimentation to scientific evaluation of all this. The science of quantum physics will support all that you do now with energy work.

"Quantum physics" will provide a way for even the most skeptical person to become a believer. Quantum is the underlying truth for the Universal Law of Attraction, which teaches that we attract into our lives whatever we focus on. Quantum Physics teaches that everything is vibrating Energy — thoughts and intentions creating on waves of energy.

By understanding that everything is Energy in a state of potential, and by applying the Law of Attraction, meaning that which is "like is drawn unto itself," man will learn again the power of intention and declaration, or of co-creation with the Source of all that exists.

If you don't like the story you are writing, you can write a new one by changing your focus and attention.

Some people, through their efforts, attract only the highest good… others still allow for the balance to swing into the negative side. But neither force is more powerful than the other. They are both necessary for the world, for human evolution.

This concept of the quantum may be difficult to understand for those faithful who are pure of heart, trusting only their religion to provide the answers. It will be difficult for those who have lived much of their life believing those translations of Spiritual teachings by religious zealots who needed power or control over others once upon a time in human history.

We sense your consternation, and so leave you with these thoughts to ponder. You two will be teaching these concepts in your work. They'll become clearer when it is time for you to truly understand their meaning.

Life is a circle, a spiral—life is not a continuum of life to death. It is a flow of systems known and unknown to man, spiraling into the cosmos. The coming of the Holy Spirit is, in part, about re-awakening to the Sacred knowledge of how spiritual energy works in all of creation.

(This is another riddle for you to solve with your colleagues and friends.)"

Sonanda Christ

I was exhausted after reading and re-reading this message. I couldn't get my mind around this explanation. I didn't fully understand the notion of nuclear physics, so quanta units or mechanics blew my mind. I did a little research, but I still didn't really get it. I just trusted that when and if it was time for me to understand, I would also be given that information. And I am still waiting.

I had glimpses, but the truth is that I felt as if we were making this up to answer some insatiable curiosity. Perhaps we knew there was more, yet we were trying to define it by the science and language we knew, and this was beyond that. The spiritual essence or science had escaped easy definitions, except in native lore. I was learning through some of my reading that the expressions of these concepts had shown up in the teachings of most global and aboriginal tribes. These "real people," as they called themselves, lived according to very simple laws of energy. This answered my earlier questions.

From the beginnings of recorded human history, there was a need to understand just these universal teachings:

• The Law of Attraction — like attracts like

• The Law of Conservation — waste not, want not

• *The Law of Abundance —there are enough resources to share for all life, and it is the misuse of resources that creates scarcity and hoarding*

• *The Law of Reciprocity—"do unto others what you wish them to do to you"—*

All of this information gave me a reason to pause and reflect. I remember thinking, 'how do I capture this in my work? How do I live this way without giving my life over to the public? How dare I think this is an answer for others?" I had so many of my own questions about the mystery of life. I wondered how on earth I could teach this, or if I should even try. The question I began to live into was, "What is the bigger contribution I can be?"

The Pyramids

April 13th, 1994

Dear Diary,

After searching for months for the right name for our business, Barry and I have settled on The Pyramid Resource Group. Clarity came after we watched Joseph Campbell, a modern mythologist, being interviewed by Bill Moyer on PBS about Campbell's book The Power of Myth [6]*. Here are the notes I scribbled from their conversation.*

The pyramid has four equal sides, and just as there are four directions on a compass, at the top of a pyramid the four sides come together at a point, and there the eye of God opens.

If you observe the back of the US dollar bill, you will find an amazing amount of powerful myth. The pyramid pictured there has 13 ranges (rows of blocks), indicating the transcendent number. There are also these historical "factoids" to consider:

Regarding 1776: = 1+7+7+6= 21 = "the age of reason"

13 states declared independence.

13 is the number of transformation.

13 attended the Last Supper – 12 apostles plus Christ

The 12 signs of the zodiac plus the Sun = 13

13 transcends the bounds of 12, the number for what is finite, what is known

13 is the number of resurrection and rebirth, of new life.

The men of enlightenment who founded our country knew all of this. On the back of the dollar bill, "Novus Ordo Seclorum" means "a new world order". "Annuit Coeptis" translates into: "He has smiled on our accomplishments." This 'indicates that the Divine Power has recognized and is happy with our work.

If you look behind the pyramid, you'll see a desert, but there are plants growing in the foreground. This represents our leaving the barrenness for the abundance. This country was created out of reason and enlightenment, not out of power or war. The eagle holds a laurel branch with 13 leaves in one talon and 13 arrows in the other. His gaze is toward the laurel, as a symbol of peaceful conversation, with the arrows to be used only in defense. Over the eagle's head, 13 stars are arranged in the shape of a Star of David. – once called "Solomon's Seal." [7]

We had a name for our company and we held long conversations at night in the home office after putting the babies to sleep. We talked about what we might build and do with our new-found excitement about the symbolism behind our transition and transformation. Over time, the goal crystallized: We would build a retreat center, one that would be a place where masters would come to teach. It would become the heart of the area, in the middle of the triangle—The Triangle area of North Carolina—our home. We had no clue as to how to get started, other than to begin working with clients who were interested in what we had to offer. Initially, that was Barry's program for teaching presentation skills. I had no idea how I would teach all that I had learned as a sales rep, a sales manager, a general manager, and a mommie person. I was stuck at a critical step of the big plan: Where was I to start? And how on earth did I think I could find the tools to build a business and a retreat center?

Email from Sharon

January 6th, 1995

Dear Diary,

Sharon has now acknowledged the possibility of physical death, putting us all in a dark place. I am sad. We all feel helpless, except for the prayers and healing we can offer. We watch as she fits newly discovered pieces into the puzzle of her life.

She has inspired so many of us. She has forced us to look at death with her, to realize our mortality — not as observers, but as participants. We have channeled messages, cooked together, held long conversations, and we've learned to do more than pray — we've learned to listen.

It is a frightening time. Our fears are no longer on the back burner and microscopic, they are "in-your-face" confronting, magnified. It seems a powerful, yet cruel, start of 1995 on one hand, and on the other, a loving jolt and embrace by Spirit. This seems to be her purpose — to take us through this walk. Sharon must have a contract to be our inspiration, to live fully for the brief breath of time we are here together. How do we — how do I, begin to thank her, love her, and help her when she has taken on so much. A Bible verse that I remember says, "No greater love has a man than he lay down his life for his friends."[8]— Obviously equally true of a woman. Maybe that is what is happening here.

Tucked into my journal, I found the following pages, which Sharon had sent me via email...one of the first emails I'd had received from anyone in this time of rapid expansion in our technologies. She had gathered these for me from her journal when she realized that she could die, as if she knew I would be the one to tell her story.

Excerpt from Sharon's Journal 1/6/95:

I feel like I've been in a tailspin since my appointment with my doctor on Wednesday. Hearing that, in his opinion, the cancer is advancing was not what I expected to hear. Once more, he told me he can't help me. For the first time during this whole process, the stark reality that I may die has hit me. It has brought up so many thoughts and questions that I don't know where to begin. The worst part about dying is leaving those you love. The actual dying process doesn't scare me. The thought of an agonizing period of pain and helplessness does.

I have not seriously considered dying because I have felt that there was a purpose for my having cancer to begin with. I felt I was going through it so I could help others through it, and make it easier for them. It never occurred to me until yesterday that maybe I have done that or that I am doing that now, and that was my purpose — that maybe in my death, others may have life. The idea that the event of my death could bring change to some that they may not have made otherwise, well this puts an entirely new twist on the whole journey.

I have also realized that "It is up to God" whether we live or not. I believe that there is a bit more involved in the process but I have come to believe and understand that it is not in our control.

Also, I realized last night another "truism." I have always felt that you have to fight for what you want in life. I don't believe that is true anymore. Life should be easy. Our desires should come easily to us. The old feeling was just a side branch of the "life is hard" attitude, (and one I am willing to let go of!)

To truly let go, "let God," is so foreign to us. It should be the most familiar. I know it is time to surrender to my guidance, whatever that is. I am now open to following my soul's purpose, whatever that is — whether it is going through a painful death, living a life dedicated to teaching others, or simply being and trusting. There is much to sort out, many tears to shed, many cries of anguish, many quiet moments — before I get there. This is my new goal, my new mission. I know that I need to face death squarely in the face and understand all that it means — how it affects life here and now. Another lesson to learn — I think this is the 'Big One!' Here I go...

After I read her letter, I felt an incredible loss, and for some unimaginable reason, I also felt envy. How could she have all these amazing insights? I wondered about what it meant to really surrender everything? I wondered what freedom might actually come from dying.

I sat alone in my room that evening, journaling to try and understand the foreign emotions about death, thinking about things I had never considered before. It made me weary. Preparing for bed, I wiped the mascara from my eyes and caught my image in the mirror, noticing the deepening lines in my face. I prayed aloud to my spirit guides and to God Himself, "I need a vacation— a fabulous dream tonight would be a welcome gift."

Now the interesting thing about talking out loud to the world of Spirit is that you never know what you are going to get if you are really ready to hear what they have to say.

So I had a dream.

Meeting HIM in my Dream

July 12th, 1995

Dear Diary,

I remember being escorted to the other side — to see what happens when we die. Everything was cast on a midnight blue palette. There were lots of spirits, lights, and stars set against the background. I saw a small being and somehow knew that I was to follow him. He looked like a comic mime with horizontal black-and-white-striped pajamas, and a red beanie with a yellow propeller. With goggles over his eyes, he was perched on a red unicycle. We (there were angels on both sides of me, one under each arm) followed him toward a huge light in front of us. There was wind in my face, and I felt I was flying. I was also laughing.

When we reached the light, we were transferred inside a huge sphere. I recall crystal stairs and catwalks, with spirits floating around. I saw Maw Maw there, but a younger version of her than I had known—taller, effervescent, maybe 26 years old. She smiled at me and led me to a garden where I met a very tall being cloaked in heavy robes. The robes were layered — brown/grey underneath with a grey translucent overcoat. His cloak shimmered as He moved. We talked for a long time, as I stood in front of Him, feeling taller myself.

He said, "Do not be weary Precious One. Earth is a beautiful place, a place that is honored and treasured among all beings in the Universe. The lessons are sometimes difficult in such a dense place, but they are very rich. Earth is the only place in the cosmos where you can consume such colorful gifts from the soil. It is the only place where you can touch another's skin, marry your energies in the art of making love, birth a baby and hold her close. Also, Earth is the only place in the universe where you find chocolate, which is the reason angels incarnate from time to time. It is the jewel among the life-bearing planets."

After we talked for a while, I felt much lighter. As I prepared to leave, I asked if He would tell me his name, and He said simply, "I am your God."

After what seemed an eternity, I responded, "That's what I thought." Then He led me through this sphere where there is always light and music. I was aware that it is the place that we go to transcend our human experiences on the way to heaven. It appears to be just another dimension away—one we can touch—one that we move in and out of every day — in our super-conscious and dream states. It's only "a few feet" above us.

I grew curious, "Are you my God and the God of all people on earth?"

"I am your God and I have many names and many faces among your fellowman. The Universe is infinite, and it is expanding. There are many things you may come to understand, in time, that are difficult to explain in ways that you can comprehend now. Dear One, this may be difficult for you to comprehend right now, but even I have a God, a creator." I stood in stunned silence for a very long time.

"Well, how on earth will I ever explain this one?"

"It will become easier for you all to understand in time. Earth is a part of my domain, part of the Kingdom of Heaven, but only a small part. We all exist in a circle of infinity — without beginning, without end. We are born through intention and language, as we are named, — 'And the Word was made flesh'...birth — death — a timeline continuum. This is very difficult to understand if you simply try to relate it to life as you know it." He nodded, as Mikael entered the sphere. I sensed that this was the end of our conversation.

There wasn't an opening in my mind for any more information. It was all a sensory explosion, an incredible idea; even in a dream state. We are born of language - God has a God - there is no beginning or end. WOW!

Mikael (again dressed in his striped pajamas) escorted me to a red roadster — hovering outside the orb, with room for only one. I studied it for a minute and said, "This is too small for us both — where do I sit?" He threw his head back and laughed, immediately transforming the roadster into a huge, open, red, trolley bus with velour seats and a large, crystal disco ball hanging behind the driver's seat.

As he drove me home, people I knew and loved, some alive now and some deceased, filled the 17 seats on the bus. I smelled Tube Rose snuff and rosewater lotion. There was laughter, music, and singing.

The entire dream was surrounded by light. It was a wild ride, wilder than any adventure I had ever been on in my waking state.

I awoke with appreciation filling my body. I was grateful to be alive and well, grateful for the experiences that had led me to this dream, grateful for a Maw Maw who gave me permission to travel in my dreams, and most grateful for chocolate.

Before my feet touched the bedroom floor, the entire dream had been captured in this journal. This one was so vivid and cinematic. I wondered about the numerology in the dream. Why 17 people? Was this a power number – 8, (1 and 7 added together)? If so, what was the message in that? I called Veronica. She enlightened me, explaining, "The number 8 in dreams indicates a state of completeness. This was your message. For you, it means not only a completion of a cycle, but I sense a completeness in your state of being, your trusting the Supreme Father/Mother God, and coming to know intimately the Almighty, the Invisible Guiding Hand."

□ ◇ □ ◇ □ ◇ □ ◇ □ ◇ □ ◇ □ ◇ □ ◇ □ ◇ □ ◇ □ ◇ □ ◇ □ ◇ □ ◇ □ ◇ □ ◇ □

The Other Side

August 20th, 1995

Dear Diary,

I drove to Duke Hospital last night and sat with Sharon for the evening. Steve needed a break. I rubbed her feet for almost two hours; I placed a cold towel on her head. The nausea appeared to rack her bones and caused her to shudder.

Her physician came in with three interns who stood looking down at the floor. The doctor told her that they were changing her medicine cocktail in her intravenous drip. She was in so much pain, her gaze didn't change at all as she appeared to stare right past them into space. I asked about what they were doing, and he said something about her needing more sodium and Pepcid to help settle her stomach. They were managing the pain. These cats were the most sober and ultra-serious people I'd ever seen. Maybe that's what working with cancer patients does to the psyche, but I had to break the maudlin moment, so I asked. "Could you just find a salt lick and let me drive her home?" She's doing swell until she comes here and you remind her she's sick." The interns looked up, and one even broke a smile, before they sulked off, leaving us in the quiet room. I kissed her forehead and sat watching her sleep.

When she came around a couple hours later, she opened her eyes and smiled. "Salt lick?" Belly laughs.

She confided to me, "I wasn't in my body when they were discussing what they were doing. I was in a space just below the ceiling, watching all of this unfold. The doctors here are wonderful people, but I swear I know why they are licensed to 'practice' medicine. It's because it's tough to get it right, to really do more than just treat symptoms and mix drugs to ease pain. We live in a disease-care state of being, not a health-care state."

Physicians are going to need to find the combined emotional and physiological reasons for disease and look beyond what they have learned strictly from a material science perspective. They are going to need to ask about nutrition and diet and what we put in our bodies and minds, including our thoughts, dreams, and fears. And, they are going to need to develop a sense of lightness to enjoy their work. Their attitudes are conveyed into the patient's healing process.

She told me later that when I rubbed her feet she started feeling herself ease back into her body. She looked like an angel, but I noticed a bump on the top of her head – something I had not seen before. Her hair was longer and she had hidden it, until now.

From Sharon's journal – a page copied and placed in mine :

8/21/95

So much has happened since my last entry. First of all, the hospital stay—I feel that during that time I was deciding whether to "stay" or "go." I felt two parts of me were debating the matter — whether you call it conscious and subconscious or whatever. I spent a lot of time outside my body in a place of incredible peace. I woke up one time and had no idea where I was. I figured out that I was in a hospital but I had no idea in what city. One night I kept hearing "Bridge Over Troubled Water" play over and over as if coming from a nearby night club. The next night I heard Moody Blues music over and over. I felt it was time for me to return to the "infant" stage. Others had to bathe me, feed me and take care of me. I allowed others to nurture me, as babies should be nurtured. In my dream I received the love and nurturing that so many offered me — Mother and Daddy, Steve, DJ and the others.

About a week after she came home from the hospital, Sharon felt sure she would heal. I gave her Reiki treatments, but she pulled no energy. In fact, her body returned the energy. It felt like there was a fan whirling between her body and my hands – it was almost as if she were giving me a Reiki treatment. The intuition I had was, "All is well." Sharon is healed, her purpose fulfilled.

Her energy and appetite returned a few days later. She had received a message in her own journal entries telling her to take a trip to England. This had given her so much to look forward to, and to plan for. It became her benchmark for declaring herself "well."

She ordered clothes for the trip and made lists of things to borrow from me. She determined the size of the suitcases she would need to pack. She made plans for the animals to be cared for and arranged for someone to check on the house. She ordered airline tickets. All the mundane things most of us do to plan a trip, she did with great enthusiasm. She loved having something to look forward to.

She experienced every step of the trip to England in a wheelchair, Steve carrying her in and out of Bed-and-Breakfast Inns. She saw Stonehenge, Big Ben, and Trafalgar Square. The inns had received her meal plans via fax or email, and they cooked dishes especially for her. This trip rejuvenated her. Yet it was also a time of revelation – this would be the last trip she would take. She related the details of this trip with reflection. In listening to her, I sensed she knew that she was experiencing living fully each day, and that this was the only promise she could claim.

She came to see this illness and her life as a big treasure hunt, and she focused on what she most appreciated about each rare, though simple, experience of each glorious day. She started her mornings by praying, focusing her attention on an altar in her new bedroom. She was sleeping in the guest room on the first level, where Steve tucked her in each night before climbing the stairs to the spacious bedroom they had spent so much time drawing into the house plans. After her ritual prayer each morning, she jotted notes in her journal and read to me. I made egg salad with olives and silken tofu one morning, and she groaned with delight when she took the first bite.

She quoted Meister Eckhart, German theologian and mystic, "If the only prayer you ever say in your whole life is "Thank You God," that would suffice." She ate more of the sandwich and between bites she added, "Appreciation is simple and brings so much joy to the heart. It's something we can all do anytime, anywhere. It seems that the Universal flow gives us more of what we most appreciate. For me, it has become so simple—more time with my friends, talking about things that matter."

Following my wise friend's lead, I started performing a ritual of appreciation every morning before my feet hit the floor. From my experience, appreciation is like a powerful magnet, drawing only good to us, accelerating the experience of miracles. It erases my fears. Whatever brings joy, whatever we are most grateful for, has an energy all its own. God seems to want to give us more of that. It's as if He is shopping for a gift for us and all we have to do is drop Him a hint.

One day that fall I had emptied the large Chinese urn planter in my bedroom of a wilted house plant, washed the hand-painted ceramic, and placed it back on the wooden stand. As I stood back and looked at it, I thought to myself, "What I would really love for that space is a tall palm." The next afternoon - the very next afternoon—a palm arrived with a big yellow bow on it, a gift from McCall, who had just been promoted to run a group of stations in Richmond. I became more aware of miracles in little things, which became miracles in bigger things. I could think of someone I hadn't heard from in a while, and they would call, sometimes within a few minutes. If I was weary from too much housework, I would think about how much time I needed to rejuvenate, and my clients would call to reschedule their impending appointments. Everything seemed to be flowing. I don't recall everything feeling easy, but I do recall it all felt like it was working.

Much of what Sharon experienced during this time was a lesson for me. She was dealing with a life-and-death conversation, while I was simply dealing with a life transition, learning to trust what life handed me. It was her brave example, though, that helped me understand the concepts of living fully. An important aspect of this lesson was learning to let go of the small stuff, like money worries, snotty noses, and the perennial quandary - what to do next.

Appreciation wasn't a new concept for me, but her gratitude for every experience, including the disease, gave me pause. I began a list of everything I could think of that I am grateful for. Naming the things I appreciated gave them new life.

My view of teaching had changed. I no longer held it out as something akin to elementary school models, with the teacher talking and the students listening. I had come to realize that true teaching involves a bigger conversation, an exploration, a modeling of how to design a life, how to find a still point to stand in and observe the world. I started noticing that I no longer had any interest in general gossip conversations. For me to be engaged, I had to be in a conversation that had meaning. The world around me was the same, but I saw it differently. I had changed a lot as I watched my dear friend.

Just Love Those I Send

October 1st, 1995

Dear Guides,

Thank You, Thank You, Thank You!

I love my life. I now work just three days a week. The new nanny, who cares for Baby Hank while I work, leaves after we meet Jess at the bus stop. I spend the rest of my time focused on the kids and Sharon, and taking classes to become a Professional Executive Coach, so I can work from home. I am more at ease than I can ever remember being. It's all working!

I'd been attending Coach U classes at night, and I worked on designing classes with Thomas Leonard, the training company's founder and President. There was an amazing group of people gathering—a new family for me—and we were participating in the most-accessible adult learning model, with every class being taught virtually. I was taking three classes from other teachers around this time and teaching two classes, most of them at night via teleconference. We prepared for our first live meeting as trainers in Ft. Lauderdale at the house of my mentor, Susan Kline, around this time, November 1995, I think.

It really was all working, and yet I was still carrying a lot of emotion in my body. I relaxed in my bathtub every night after putting the kids to bed. With the candles lit, I breathed deep, cleansing breaths and tried to stay focused in my meditations. I imagined the word "empty" crossing my mind, closing my eyes to see it written, as if on a blackboard. I waited for the thoughts of the day to stop rolling in and out of the picture, staying with it until I found my still point. I would then ask a question and wait for the answer.

One night during this period of time, I asked the recurring question, the one I was growing weary of, but the one on my mind — and Sharon's — and the minds of the dozen clients I had begun to work with in some way. Some of these clients were former radio clients bartering clothing, and some were former broadcaster colleagues who really wanted my help. They had hired me as their "coach," which was part of the educational model. We had to build a business and practice with clients. The nagging question that kept me –and many of them, I suppose—awake at night was…

"What's next? What am I to do now?"

The answers were coming faster now, as I was getting into the practice of finding my center, asking a question, and waiting patiently for an answer.

"Dear Daughter,
Just love the people I place in front of you."
That was it.

I waited for more. Nothing came.

I sat in my tub staring at candles, empty of thoughts, grounded in the water until it got cool. I pulled the brass stopper and allowed myself to sit and feel heavy as the water spiraled down the drain, leaving the tub and me to grow cold together.

When I stood up and wrapped a big white fluffy towel around me, I caught a glimpse of my form in the mirror. There was a shadow behind me—a beaming shadow with wings. I turned around quickly, hoping to catch a glimpse of the face of what I felt was an angel. Nothing there.

"Well, loving people is something I can do," I declared out loud, realizing that goose bumps covered my body.

I had three new clients by the end of the next day, all out-of-the-blue referrals from someone who had heard about the new work I was doing. I smiled as I pulled the kids in the Radio Flyer wagon after dinner that same night. "It'll be alright—have a good time," rolled through my brain.

A Re-Membering

June 11th, 1996

Dear Diary,

It's my birthday! I have been celebrating since June 1st, the start of an entire month of lunches with friends, something fun every day. The best gift so far today was a visit with Hank this morning while he watched me apply make-up. He sat in my bathroom, perched on the toilet, chatting away about a dream, so I wrote it in his journal. Here's how our "chat" went.

(Hank) "Mom, I had a remembering last night."

(Me) "You mean you had a dream?"

(Hank) "No, more like a re-membering. Mom, if you are a little boy in this lifetime, were you a little boy in the last one?"

(Me) "Do you mean, you are a little boy now, so were you a little boy before you came to Earth? Or do you mean, you are a little boy now so were you a little boy in another life here at another time?"

(Hank) "I mean another time, but my skin was more colorful." He rubbed his fat almost-four-year-old fingers from his right hand down his left arm to show me.

(Me) "Oh, how colorful were you?"

(Hank) "I was about as black as your shoes," he stated, as he pointed to my patent leather pumps.

(Me) "So, was I your mom?" I was actually curious to know if I was a part of this dream.

(Hank) "No, but she was a really nice lady. Mom, I was a big, beautiful black man, and I liked to play music on a round guitar."

He went on to chatter about how he liked to eat cooking like my Mom makes, "country flavors," he said. I picked him up and hugged him so tight I thought his eyes might pop out, gathered his sister, who was dressing herself in one of her most lovely dresses, not willing to wear pants to school yet, and made my way gently into my day.

I smiled all day ...thinking about what an amazing gift it was to be a mother.

Hank and Jessica were always surprising me with stories, challenging me to see things in a fresh way. My children did come to teach me. I was struck at the time with thoughts of what might be possible if we could all see our evolution as a process of wearing different "skin"—sometimes a different gender, sometimes a more-colorful body, sometimes a less-colorful one.

Permission

September 12th, 1996

Maw Maw,

This past year has been a blur. The kids are doing well, and business is growing. I am getting a lot of speaking dates, and many of them involve travel, so it's been difficult to keep up with the writing. Sharon's health is beginning to really decline. She has been so brave with this illness for so long.

What should I do for her now?

"Write her a note giving her permission to leave you. Sometimes, it is the permission and the forgiveness and the promise of forever we need in order to let go of our human body. I stayed in my own body long after it served me, because I wanted to make sure everyone had time to say good-bye. It is difficult, when you love your life, to accept dying.

When you let go, so will she.
  I will meet her on the other side."
    Love, Maw Maw

My Dearest Sharon,

"I sense it is time for you to rest with God. Your work is complete. Thank you for guiding us to the place of deeper understanding and acceptance. We know more about the gift of life, because you have lived with us. Please don't stay here for us any longer. It is better for you to transition now than to stay longer and suffer more. We are ready - all of us. Be at Peace. Go with our Love. We will all see you on the other side."

Your Pal Forever,

        DJ

I cried when I found this note. This was when I began to say good-bye to my dear friend, knowing that she would leave soon. I wondered if I had been selfish and insensitive in thinking that I was the one who needed to give her permission to leave us all. I second-guessed my intentions. Was I the one who needed freedom from the stresses that her illness and care had brought to those around her? Was I insincere in my sentiment that I wanted to have my dear friend let go and find her peace? Hadn't she been there, unselfishly with me, guiding me into my own inner workings so I could learn my life lessons for this time and space?

See Ya Later

October 15th, 1996

My Dear Guides,

Steve called me today to tell me it's time to come say my good-byes to Sharon. I arrived at the house to see butterflies dancing in the butterfly garden he had planted in the middle of their circle drive. Although he claimed the project was just "something to keep his hands busy," I knew it was a work of his heart — it was in the direct view of Sharon's bedroom window. She'd spent the past year in that bed, reading and journaling, often surrounded by the friends who cared for her in every way, from bathing her to cooking for her to feeding her.

When he greeted me, it was obvious he'd already spent some time saying his own good-byes. I looked deep into his eyes and caught the sadness, weariness, and pain. The hospice worker counted out enough meds for one more day, packed her things, and left. Steve said nothing, but escorted me back through the massive kitchen, down the hall, past the concrete Quan Yin statue, into the cool sea-green guest bedroom that she'd claimed over a year ago. I entered the room and stopped near the foot of the bed, touching her legs. The altar with a lithograph of Jesus caught the sunlight in the room.

Steve pointed over her head to the ceiling and explained that she was "hanging out up there," smiled as he touched my shoulder, and left us.

I looked up toward the ceiling, softly held her feet to ground myself, and starting talking, "Hello, my Dearest Friend. You have decided to go, I see. I will miss your laughter, your hugs, your smart-ass comments — I mean wisdom." I have no idea what else I said, except, "See you later — I will definitely live well in case the birds are watching me — taking messages to God and Santa, and so I promise to see you later!"

I just stood there in disbelief that this beautiful soul was leaving. She had become a part of me. I knew I would carry her essence, her story, with me forever.

"Go rest. Go play with the angels," I'd finished, after I realized how empty everything sounded.

I walked into the living room and melted into Steve's shoulder. He escorted me to the kitchen, where she had handwritten her last wishes, her will, in a composition book, and he pointed to the first line of the section about her service.

DJ will do the Eulogy.

I was overwhelmed with emotion. What could I say that would capture her story?

I left after weeping into Steve's shoulder. Not prepared for visits with the others who were driving in to say their own good-byes, I just sat in the car for a few minutes, watching the butterflies. I felt as if I had fallen off a tall building and had the wind knocked out of me. I took a deep breath, put the car into gear, and inched away down the winding gravel drive.

Then it hit me: "Oh my Lord. Barry's 40th birthday is Sunday. We're supposed to be in the Keys for his fishing trip with a guide this weekend." Logistics danced across my mind until I parked them in a "to do" box in my brain where I could retrieve them later. I think women always go into the logistics of taking care of others in a crisis—but I was grieving. I needed to just be in my sadness.

Six young deer traipsed across my path on my way out of the rural neighborhood. I stared at a young doe that stopped in the middle of the road, unafraid, soulful. I looked at her, and she seemed to smile before running like a gazelle through the woods with the others following her lead.

I drove out of the backwoods and turned onto the old state road. I opened the sunroof and turned on the radio. "It will be alright— have a good time," —the remake by Huey Lewis and the News, started to play. The radio was tuned to a country station. The song wasn't on that playlist.

I laughed out loud.

The next morning I woke up to a beautiful sunny day, said

a prayer of gratitude, and started making my bed. I stopped at the foot of the bed and felt Sharon's spirit swirl like a warm, strong breeze of energy radiating from my feet and moving through my body, leaving the top of my head with a sensation of being on fire. Ten minutes later, a friend called from her house, but I already knew she was gone. An instant later I smelled the strong aroma of Tube Rose snuff, and I knew Maw Maw was there in spirit to comfort me, to let me know that my friend was in guiding hands.

I sat at the bottom of the bed knowing my life had just changed. The time and energy that I shared with her would be refocused. Yet I knew that many things would never be replaced. I mourned the end of spiritual conversations that were ours alone, the shared time in that space where all aspects of our worlds collided and allowed us contemplation.

In addition to directing me to give her eulogy, Sharon had also willed that a couple of other gal pals and I go shopping in her closet and take anything we could wear – we all wore the same size. Many times, when we thought she needed a shopping fix, we'd sat on her bed, paging through catalogs, pretending to buy anything we wanted. Occasionally she would find something that would make her light up, and it would appear in a brown box a few days later, a gift. I asked Steve to put one outfit "on layaway," the one I would wear for her funeral. It was an outfit I had chosen as a reward for her when she was the sales person of the month, not long after she had first joined the radio staff.

Two days later, with the ashes of her cremated body in a Raku urn she had chosen as the centerpiece on the altar, we gathered in her home church in Sanford to remember our dearest friend.

She had written a note to us all and had rolled copies of it into tiny scrolls. I began the eulogy by reading it.

"My Dear Friends and Family,

"I want you all to know how much I love you and how much I appreciate all of your love and support that you have so freely given me. Your prayers and your love gave me energy; your hugs gave me warmth, your smiles brought me fun and laughter."

I felt a tug at my skirt, which gave me pause in the reading. No, it was Sharon's skirt. I was wearing her clothes to comfort me — and as a reminder not to be too serious. The jacket was red with Chinese patterns and brass studs; almost garish — just the item she would have wanted me to wear. Then there was another set of tugs . . . three of them. No one else was around me. I had not caught the skirt on anything. These were definitely tugs. I felt something else at play also. As I spoke, the voice was mine, but the energy was hers. I spoke with a passion and a peace that could have only come from someone in another state of being: it was a spiritual frequency not my own. She was present in spirit in a way that I had never experienced—she was literally speaking through me.

I stopped for a moment to catch my breath and gaze into the eyes of her beloved friends and family. I breathed the deepest breath of my life and, finding my center, I continued.

"Please do not be sad. I am now in a place of love, peace and joy. We will be together again. I will always be with you in spirit and I hope that a small part of me lives within each of you. Please do not try to hold on to me, but release me to enter the spiritual world where we all experience the freedom and peace that we seek. My words of wisdom; Live each day to the fullest, be in the present moment, allow God to work through you and laugh at least one belly laugh every day! Love Always – Sharon"

I continued the service after the long pause. I had thankfully written the words I would say for this service in one of my journals.

She told us all more than once over the past few years, "I am not afraid of dying, but I don't think I have accomplished what I came here to do."

I assure you she accomplished much more than she could know. She rose above this disease and through her perspective about living and dying, all of us who were her friends, colleagues, and family have gained our own.

In providing this type of perspective, she gave us insight about so much that happens in life, and through this wisdom and new view we began to see miracles in the world.

We spent time philosophizing during our daily conversations. We mused that before we were born we were getting our assignments for this earth school experience while seated in a large circle in one of the many rooms of heaven. God paused and carefully looked around the room then asked for a volunteer who was up for a big challenge. Being naturally courageous, Sharon raised her hand right away. "Alright, Pick me. Pick me. I'll take the tough assignment." During our walks through the mountains, she asked me several times to promise to sit on her hands the next time God gave out assignments about courage, and this statement was always followed by a belly laugh.

Here's what we discovered in our quest over the past few years.

There is a potential miracle in everything that happens

We are always either living or dying

As for the first revelation, a potential miracle in everything that happens, we chose to adopt this view to see possibilities. If there is a miracle or a purpose in everything that happens, then we just might trust the challenges we face as if they are ordained—maybe even predestined. If there is a miracle in everything that happens, maybe we can maintain a sense of humor in seemingly humorless situations. If we could see our lives as a coursework in which we are simply the learner, then in the space of learning it is possible to experience daily miracles.

Many people stay in jobs, relationships, careers, companies, countries, and states of mind because at some mental level they are afraid of dying—or losing someone or something they hold dear. Sharon wasn't afraid of death.

At no time in the three years of radical chemo treatments, of holistic healing approaches, or of spiritual seeking and healings, did she ever speak about fearing death. She wanted to live, and live fully. She wanted to live in the beautiful home she and Steve built on the Haw River in Pittsboro, centered in ten acres of woods.

As for the second revelation, one of our friends said about her when I declared she was dying in the last few months—"no, she is living, she has always been living." Even though she accepted that life and the desire to live on this beautiful land was temporary, she continued to live fully each day.

So we all began asking, "What would happen—or what would change—if, like Sharon, we weren't afraid of dying?" The answers led us to new careers, new choices about where we lived, and more loving and intimate connections with those precious to us.

"Sharon's final message was about living, not dying—I think this is what she wanted me to say to you in summary:

Love each other:

I can tell you the time we spent together, she and this motley group here today, was about love, a precious love, a 'tough, we can handle anything together' kind of love. And she brought out the best in us—the love in us—because she entered these conversations in the workplace, in her home, and in her daily communications.

Sharon thought genuine love is the only reality we need to know. It gives us perspective and helps us see miracles in our most challenging experiences.

Live out Loud:

Sharon Crone blazed her own path. She found her purpose—to teach us to create our own legacies, that we can make choices that are aligned with our gifts and live according to what we most want to do and be, that we need not fear the future, the disease, the unknown, but can embrace every precious moment. The future is only a series of present moments.

Laugh a Belly Laugh:

Sharon's laugh came from her toes and her gut, and it was contagious. Everyone who knew her had stories they could share of fun times together, even in the last months and weeks of her life. Here's one that exemplifies her sense of humor.

Sharon and I were spending our lunch one day at a bookstore in downtown Durham soon after she had been diagnosed, and we happened on some copper pyramids, the ones that are supposed to hold a magic energy. You can place bread under these and it is supposed to stay fresh for two weeks. You can put wilting plants under these and they will regenerate. So we bought two, one for each of us.

On the way out of the store we simultaneously put them on our heads and walked back to the car to drive to the office. Two stoplights into our drive, a police car pulled up beside us. Sharon looked at the officer, who was obviously questioning what planet we were from, looked back at me and said, 'Well, you would think he had never seen two women in a black shiny car with pyramids on their heads before!'

Belly Laugh and perspective!

She celebrated my fortieth birthday by reminding me that when I took life (or myself) too seriously, I must remember that she—and a couple of police officers with my license plate number—had seen me with a pyramid on my head!" I will remember those words when life seems hard or when I take myself too seriously. Perspective!

I think Sharon would want us to see her in a state of "well-being." Perhaps we need to all recognize that Sharon has been well in spirit all along.

Please repeat each of these statements as we recall a message from A Course in Miracles [9]:

I can see peace instead of pain and grief,
All is well!
I can see the full miracle of Life!
All is well!
There is nothing to fear in the world!

All is well!
Sharon is well!
All is well.
Amen and Amen.

The service ended shortly after this conclusion. I almost levitated. One of our friends walked up to me and said, "Girlfriend, I don't know what you have been doing lately, but you need to stop and go get yourself a church!" I kept telling people that what they heard was not from me and that Sharon was there. They kept patting me on the back, telling me I had delivered a great tribute. The experience was surreal.

I settled more fully into my body on the way home in the family van with Barry, as we discussed the rescheduled 40th birthday trip for him to the Keys to go fishing. My mind danced in circles between the trip to play in the water—one I so needed—and my reflections of Sharon.

In aboriginal tribes, the crone was the wisest elder woman whom others sought for story-telling and spiritual teachings. The crone was also the miracle worker, the **mystic**. Sharon gained this name literally in her marriage to her soul mate companion. She lived as the elder among this tribe of colleagues, family members and friends, and so it was fitting that she left the planet with this name.

I had just rather absent-mindedly said, "See you later," aloud to her while saying my good-byes, but I was growing confident she had taken my sentiment quite literally as she continued to show up.

She hung out in my bathroom, where I would sometimes hear her laughter as I put on my make-up for the day. It was her voice that I often heard in my head at critical times, asking me, "So what are you afraid of this time, Precious Darelyn? What are you really afraid of Dragon Lady?" And when I heard her in my mind, I knew that hers was a playful voice of reason, reminding me that death of the ego and the body is inevitable, but that learning to live well would continue to be my greatest challenge.

She reminded me to live out loud!

After the funeral we ceremoniously shared our favorite stories about our dear family member and friend, as we grieved her passing from the material world and celebrated her passage into the spirit realm.

Beginning that autumn, we used the Crone's house for a retreat center for awhile—for gal pal weekends and healing circles. We called one of these gatherings the "Wild Woman's Woo Woo Weekend," where my other dear gal pals were encouraged to bring their unique talents and gifts— stories, yoga exercises, palm reading, nail painting, cooking—whatever felt right for them to contribute. At one point during this first retreat, we girls were all sitting outside for dinner, quietly eating healthy food and watching wildlife meander through the mature woods. Without the slightest breeze, the wooden wind chime hanging from the eaves above my head, a gift I'd given Steve and Sharon for the house-warming, went wild, shaking and ringing as if it were being blown about by a storm. We all stopped eating and chatting and just looked at each other. It stopped cold still and I laughed out loud, practically singing, "Hi Sharon!" It chimed acknowledgement, then stopped cold again.

June 11th, 1997

Dear Maw Maw and Sharon,

It is my 41st birthday, and it has been awhile since I wrote to you. I think I needed a recovery period, if not a time of assimilation of information from all the journaling and messages gleaned over the past few years. As usual, my birthday is being celebrated as a month-long event, including the traditional lunches — one per day - with my gal pals, playing hooky from work to have lunch with one of the kids, and shopping when I feel like it. Barry is taking us all to a ballgame tonight, where I plan to eat a big, fat hotdog—or a Flying Burrito—or maybe both!

Sharon — is that you showing up in my shower?

"Yes, my dear. That is where you are most grounded—in the water. I can also hear your laughter and your questions more clearly when you are there. You will notice I have been showing up with questions instead of some fabulous insight or fashion advice. Questions are the keys to unlocking the most powerful answers — 'your own.'

Maw Maw and I are with you. We are working with your other guides—

I didn't tell anyone that I still had visits from Sharon, or that Maw Maw visited me in my dreams and when I was in the yard playing with the kids, as she moved in and out of trees in the woods around us. I settled into the acceptance that I had to live in a way that would bridge these two worlds when the time came. At that time I was just happy to still be in communication, to be at-one with both of them.

Collard Greens & New Intentions

The collard greens are in the crock pot, and the pork roast is in the oven. My mother's Bar-B-Que (ketchup, vinegar, brown sugar and lemon) dip is cooking on the stove, and the sweet potatoes have been boiled to make yam casserole with a toasted marshmallow topping. I love the traditional New Year's Day meal—the black-eyed peas and collards that represent pennies and green backs, symbols of good fortune consumed after a blessing for all of our relations and the abundance we experience every day.

Today, as I sat to write my intentions for the year, I caught a glimpse of Maw Maw—and then one of Sharon. Both appeared younger and even more beautiful than when I knew them.

I wondered for a minute what they were doing here, so I asked in the journal:

Hey — What are you girls up to?

"We are here to dine with you. We came for the feast and the aromas that travel through space into heaven. We know you love cooking — and this is your smoke signal for all of us on the other side.

We stand around the dining table when we hear your laughter and get a whiff of the scents from your kitchen. On this side, we see the light in your halo expand when you are in the joy of preparing food for your body, and sharing stories with friends around your table to nurture the spirit.

Know that we are still with you. There is a beautiful and powerful group of guides who are hovering around you, ready for deployment as you capture your intentions to guide our energies."

With Our Love and Light
Maw Maw and Solara

Intentions for 2001

• Travel to some cool places — I already know I will be traveling to Switzerland in May and Japan in November, both written prophecies from my journals

• Have the business continue to thrive - -

- Donate some major money to a worthy cause that benefits children

- Spend fun times with family

- Write my book...Mystic GRITS is the name I keep getting.

As I continued to write, other guides came to me with answers to my questions and comments on my musings and reflections.

My reflection about the work I do this year gave me this insight and question: So much of the work I am doing is closet "woo-woo." So, dear guides, will there be a time when there is a more widely accepted conversation about the awareness of loving others and our connection to the world of spirit, even in the corporate work we do?

"Dear One,

You are playing a bigger game than you know when you are in the course of working with individual leaders and their teams. You are playing a business game, which is the ultimate game within the game. This means that you are meeting many people who live and work in a state of fear, so you have been and will continue to work with them on many levels—Connecting, Awakening, and Teaching. The first level is to connect them with their individual power and to help them name their strengths and gifts, as well as identify their fears and illusions. In this way you may be reawakening them to their soul's purpose, or giving them access to their soul's story as it appears in the records for all times... the Akashic Records. You've probably noticed that people often tell you that when they work with you, something magical happens, and they feel peaceful. This is because in the space of your conversation you connect them to their voice of wisdom and purpose, a voice which conquers fear and invites them to move with courage. The second level is that you are awakening them to a higher calling, even in the context of the way they do business now. Your partnership helps facilitate the falling away of greed, ego, and mandated business goals, so that each person's highest and best is at play — each person realizes a meaningful contribution. On the third level, when you work with their teams, you are giving the entire group access to a functional wisdom—you are teaching and conveying the simple, yet essential implementation of communication skills that honor the conscious awakening. In this way, you are teaching them to express their individual purpose and honor their spiritual pathways within the context of the team's focus. If people cannot soar personally, they will feel like victims and will be lost in their search to contribute their many gifts and serve in ways that are more aligned with their soul's blueprint.

You must know that this is a time of planetary shifts, and the first place that you will witness these shifts will be in business. Some still need to exercise power by taking more of the resources than is needed, and this will cause an imbalance. This is always an indicator of the spiritual evolution or disintegration of a society. Things will get better and better as companies become more aligned in service to the human spirit of *their employees and customers. Conversely, things will become worse and worse when there is a lack of attention to this spiritual alignment. You are beginning to witness this truth now on a large scale.*

You will be translating the work of the Angel Mikael group, which is ultimately the message of love and mercy. You may never need to call attention to the fact that this is what you are doing unless there is an opening to do so. It will be understood at a deep cellular level by those who are ready to awaken to their own heart callings. This is a critical time for Y-O-U-R (O-U-R) work, and there are many who were born at this time to play in our "game" on Earth. The ultimate "goal" of this extraordinary game is the evolution of the human spirit to a place of deeper knowing, trusting, and partnership in creation.

I noticed when I completed writing these pages how the language jumped off the page. The fact that "YOURS" is actually mostly "OURS" set my mind dancing, and it awakened me to how unconscious we have become to the power of language—the power of words, and the power of synchronicity. [10]

Sonia

May 17th, 2001

Dear Guides,

Please tell me about Sonia. I had an interesting encounter on my trip to Grindlewald, Switzerland, yesterday. This is one of the most awe-inspiring and beautiful places I have ever seen, and everything about this trip has felt magical so far.

So what should I know about my traveling companion Sonia?

"Dear Precious One,

Sonia is wisdom. You were visited by wisdom, herself."
The Girls!

Sonia was the last person to board the Swiss Air flight from New York to Zurich. She stood about four-and-a-half-feet tall, wore a dark-pink/red raincoat, and carried a simple tote. She took the only seat available, the one next to mine. I had begun to think that I would be able to stretch a bit on the overnight flight to Europe, but instead I received the gift of Sonia's company.

I helped Sonia buckle her seat belt and get settled as we prepared for our dinner and the movie "Chocolat."

"What takes you to Switzerland?" I inquired.

"I am going to celebrate my 85th birthday with my sisters. They are turning 92 and 94 this week." Her eyes twinkled as she told me this news.

"What's the best part about turning 85?"

"The best part of turning 85 is that I no longer care what people think of me. I do the work I want to do…I am a volunteer candy-striper at a hospital in New York City. And I am still learning, see?" From her tote she pulled a Microsoft course-completion certificate, which she planned to show her sisters. I am free to go anywhere I want and do anything I choose."

Then she asked me, "What takes you to Zurich?"

"I am going to preside over the first-ever international coaching conference. I am a coach and president of the International Organization of Coaches."

She asked me to explain coaching, and I gave her a few definitions, settling on the theme that all coaching is designed to be a partnership focused on helping people to create the life of their dreams, doing the work they are called to do, discovering meaning.

She looked at me the way Maw Maw often did and said simply, "Coaching is too harsh a word for what you do. What you do is guide people to their inner wisdom before they are 85 years old. You should call yourself a "guide."

I used that story to open the conference. There were people there from 68 different countries, speaking many languages. My opening address was interpreted in five languages on stage, as I told this story in small chunks. The blessing I received in part was that I was able to hear my story conveyed with the lilt and emotion of the interpretations. I saw how this story landed in the facial expressions of many cultural representatives.

I think I have had only a glimpse of just how significant this encounter was with Sonia. She gave me new language for my work as a coach – I was to be a guide to my clients' inner wisdom.

What I didn't include in that diary entry was something that happened after we departed the plane to process through customs. Sonia took a turn just outside the concourse and disappeared. She claimed no bags, though she had told me she planned to stay for a few weeks.

When I recently repeated this story to a friend of mine who studies mysticism, he gave me another possible way of understanding this experience.

He wrote to me in an email response to my sharing of this story in the summer of 2008:

Oh my goodness, DJ!!! Do you know who you were visited by? The name Sonia is a variant of Sophia!!! Sophia is Wisdom. Are you familiar with Gnosticism? Sophia is the incarnation of the transcendent god's wisdom. Sophia is the mediating power between the higher spiritual reality and the illusory worldly "reality". Sophia leaves the spheres of Truth to enter into the world of Lies and redeem us by reminding us of our greater nature. THAT is who sat next to you on the plane!"

The first clue, other than her name, is her age, 85. These digits add up to 13, and 13 is an extraordinarily meaningful number. The number 12 represents a sacred cycle, and 13 is the first step in the new sacred cycle. And then there are the ages of her "sisters." When you add the digits of her 92-year-old "sister," you get 11. The number 10 represents a worldly cycle, and 11 is the beginning of a new worldly cycle. Then consider the 94-year-old "sister," whose digits add up to 13! Her oldest older "sister's" age signifies the ancient sacred cycle of 13; her other older sister's age signifies the worldly cycle we are just completing, and Sonia herself said she is 85, signifying a new sacred cycle ready to begin.

And the proof of this? She shows you her Microsoft certification. Sophia has learned Technology. Wisdom and Technology are ready to integrate! This is truly amazing.

DJ, I know this all sounds like gobbledygook to you, but I don't usually go off like this. I tend to keep my mysticism hidden. But, whether Sonia was a vision or an actual person, the symbolism of your story just shouted out to me. Through this experience, the Wisdom in the Universe was giving you a profound message.

Your friend, Label

I met Label Braun a month prior to sharing this story at the <u>Conversation Among Masters</u> coaching conference in Asheville, NC. I have learned to trust those chance encounters I have with people who are tuned to the same frequencies. He was one of those. I wasn't looking for confirmation, but his interpretation was an example of the many I have had throughout my life. Seems my teachers, guides, and friends have a habit of showing up with just the right information just in time, and whenever I need it most. His message was another spark for my completing this work.

Label traveled to see me and I read him some of what I was writing at the time. He asked me to send a copy to him, which I refused to do, as I was still hesitant about how all this information might land among those I most love. He started asking me about the book every couple of weeks by leaving a phone message or sending me an email. I realized after a few conversations that this wizard was also holding the space for this book to become a reality. Another new guide had entered my life.

Writing—
The End or the Beginning?

February 4th, 2008

Dear Guides,

What am I to write?

"Dear One,

Your story. Start writing now. This is what you were born to do!
You are the only person who can tell your story. So get crackin'!"
Your brotherhood from the light!

My dear coach colleague and friend Harriett Simon Salinger gave me a "gift" session with a soul intuitive from NYC as a birthday gift. Two weeks later, I had another gift session, this one courtesy of my wonderful and dear old friend, Eddie Conner. Within the first few minutes of these conversations both asked me in different ways, "Where is your book?"

Each time, I heard myself start making excuses, and each time I was cut short with the message, "Start writing. Start writing, right now. This is your gift. This is what you were born to do."

And then, of course, my gal pal Sharon checked in with this entry in my journal after the first 1,400 pages of "GRITS" were written and I still didn't have a book. I did have her diaries and journals however. Steve had brought a box full of her precious journals to me, requesting that I keep them sacred and return them "when I was finished." I promised I would. The next time I sat down and started writing, the floodgates of love and emotion opened up, and so did Sharon with this message.

"Dear Friend,

Life is a sensuous experience, an ethereal dance of touch, taste, sound, and light; it is to be embraced, relished.

I hear your prayers of gratitude, and I carry blessings to your super-conscious self from your brethren on the spiritual plane. You are blessed and need to be open to receive the gifts of your writing.

It is time — BEYOND TIME — for you — to complete this book. Focus, focus, focus--this is not Hocus Pocus. Ha-ha-ha! The green journal was the journal I meant for you to have. I gave you my story, as your grandmother gave you hers.

I want you to know that we carry our discoveries, our conversations and our life lessons into the afterlife, into the next stage.

We tend to think that our minds live in our brains, but the truth is this — our memories, our minds are alive in our souls, encoding the events of each day we live on earth in life's sacred record. These records include the experience of Earth, and of all of our incarnations for all time.

That's why it's important to breathe deeply for clarity. The mind — wisdom — is accessed through the heart of your soul. When our soul's heart feels joy, our emotions signal our brains as our internal guidance system to draw unto us more of these experiences.

Fear keeps us from joy. Fear exists only in your mind, in those recent thoughts of scarcity that park themselves in your smallest human brain and stay there to keep you company when you least need it.

Do not fear sharing these stories. Feel the joy of your writing.

Be quiet, my dear friend. Find that still point from which the Universal Wisdom flows, and there you will find the strength to write.

You are music to me. When you seek me, I hear a chime that resonates throughout the heavens. Your prayers, requests, intentions, and spiritual thoughts travel as if you have called with *a signature bell. I am here, waiting for you to call me.*

Trust. That is my message to you. Trust yourself. Trust your family. Trust your friends. Trust your clients. Trust your angels and spiritual guides. Trust your God. Trust me and your precious Maw Maw.

I am now, and always will be, with you — throughout infinity."

           Solara

My view now about Writing as an act of Faith

Awaken the Torchbearers

The souls of people, on their way to Earth-life, pass through a room full of lights; each takes a taper – often only a spark – to guide it in the dim country of this world. But some souls, by rare fortune, are detained longer – have time to grasp a handful of tapers, which they weave into a torch. These are the torch-bearers of humanity – its poets, seers and saints, who lead and lift the race out of darkness, toward the light. They are the law-givers and saviors, the light-bringers, way-showers and truth-tellers, and without them, humanity would lose its way in the dark.

   –PLATO (CA. 427–CA 347 BC) GREEK PHILOSOPHER

Catholic priest, sociologist and author Andrew Geeley calls America a "nation of closet mystics." I have been one of those. There are far too many stories for me to have shared within these pages, so I selected a series that might prompt you to take time for your own exploration, by yourself or with your close friends or in book clubs. It is apparent to me that we are being called to witness a new revelation on this planet. I don't feel that it means the end of the world, the way some interpret the Bible's Book of The Revelation, but I sense it is the end of a current society. I believe it's time to step out on Faith that this calling is Divine and that the world is ready for the real work we were destined to do as coaches, philanthropists, teachers, leaders, psychics, healers, guides, gurus, authors, poets, and artists. And, as Plato wrote, it is time for those "poets, seers and saints [to] lead and lift the race."

As a professional coach and leadership consultant, I witness people creating the extraordinary every day in their quests to find meaning, both at work and as they create legacies in their communities and with their families.

I also have had the experience of having many of those people sharing their spiritual inquiries within the context of my work in business, and while I am clear that there is a time and place for every conversation—which I also learned from those clients who are atheists and agnostics—I have found people are becoming more aware and articulate of their own conscious awakenings. So it doesn't really matter to me what we call this time.

In writing this story, I became clear that I have built my life on faith, and that my faith started in my religious tradition and in my home. So, while I have journeyed down different pathways, acquiring and assimilating new information that guides my life, I have found that I am drawn to the smell of candles burning and the music of a pipe organ. I love to sing. I love to pray. I love to listen and meditate. So I am home in a house of worship, just as I am home wherever my travels have taken me. I have found peace in my own center, that still point inside that allows me to consciously choose what I will do and how I will be, day to day. Perhaps that's point of coming to Earth school – to grow spiritually, as we design our own life.

I haven't built a center for enlightenment or pyramid, as I had been told I would. Who knows, maybe I will someday. The vision of it still swims through my mind before I go to sleep. What I've learned about spiritual guidance is that as we receive information from others, we have a responsibility for discerning what will serve the highest and best in each choice we make. We have the free will to interpret what is true for us and take action on that.

There are many of us connecting every day in synchronistic and rigorous inquiries about what it means to be fully human. We are collectively asking and answering the quintessential question, "Why are we here?" and we crave meaning in our lives as we take on this enormous shift in consciousness and energy.

I feel a sense of urgency to share my story now. It feels to me that a major gateway has been opened in the past two years and the times are calling to us: " Awaken the others, and get going! You have a garden to tend and creative masters here as children to nurture. It is time for the age of enlightenment."

I am passing on the call for us to wake up and contribute to our human evolution. We are being called to tell the truth and be courageous.

You are being asked to leverage the gems from your past and consciously author a new chapter in our collective journey. By holding this story, you are being charged with going forward to shine your own light.

So now as this story ends, a new story begins.

Yours:

ACKNOWLEDGEMENTS

▫ ◇ ▫ ◇ ▫ ◇ ▫ ◇ ▫ ◇ ▫ ◇ ▫ ◇ ▫ ◇ ▫ ◇ ▫ ◇ ▫ ◇ ▫ ◇ ▫ ◇ ▫ ◇ ▫ ◇ ▫ ◇ ▫ ◇ ▫

GRATITUDE . . . For my life partner, Barry Mitsch, with deep appreciation for your gift of patience as the writer within took her sweet time awakening. To my parents for giving me a foundation of faith, and Nikki, Billy, and Terry for the stories and laughter we share about growing up in Welcome. To Steve Crone—there are no words big enough, but I hope you know how much I cherish this journey with you. To Veronica Vela for your mastery in teaching and your healing touch! To Laura Berman Fortgang for playing with me—encouraging me—and becoming the Matzoball partner for my Grits! To my gal pals— Ali Ciampa, Anita Ketcham, Cari Newton, Casey Bastian, Denise Poll, Erin McLaughlin, Karen Mills, Honorable Kristin Ruth, Lynn Godwin, Marianna Clampett, Marilyn Blankinship, Sheila Hale Ogle, Suguna Fowler, Tracey Richards, Wendy Dawson, Kathy Darr, Kathy Wilkerson, and Kathy Walker—all southern mystics at heart, especially to Wendy for the stay at Turtle Soup, and to Denise who travels in many ways with me. For the Master Coaches of the Pyramid Resource Group whose work created the space for me to write—your work lights the path for many to discover their soul's work and higher purpose—Barbara Poole, Bobbi Gemma, Brent Brower, Eileen Brown, Marianna Clampett Dr. Jeff Spar, Joe Diab, Kathy Baske Young, Kathy Faller, Dr. Marcia Reynolds, Doug Leland, Harriett Simon Salinger, Doug Silsbee, Tim Link, Carl Sharperson—without you I could only do small things. To Eddie Conner for helping me "re-member" who I am! To Tom Bensman for your loving edits and "belief!" To Jill Wright for coaching me to find my voice as a writer. To Michael and Sharon Williams for having faith in me. To Jim Curtan for your spiritual direction. To Dana Melvin, Marilyn Blankinship, Label Braun, Steve McCall for allowing me to use your stories. To Star "Sharon"

Capehart who is most entertaining and informative. To Bob Dumas and Mike Stiles, the zany radio show hosts who allowed free-spirits to play on the air at G-105. To Kitty Kinnin for inviting me to join the ranks of free spirits. To Jim Goodmon for bringing me to Raleigh and making Capitol Broadcasting one of the stellar places to work and find my way. To Carl Venters and Jack McCarthy for challenging me to bloom as an "HPW"—High Powered Woman! To Rick Kasper and Dave Hughey for trusting me with The Herald Sun Radio stations. To Mom Ruth who gave me Barry and a renewed passion for reading. To George Habel for believing and praying. To the magnificent clients who have given me the gift of "coaching" you. To Susan Klein and Shirley Anderson for mentoring me as a professional coach. To Sandy Vilas for Coach U.

To Brian Johnson and his company of greats at LOUDEST ink who "get it!"—the vision, potential, hope—and brought to life this body of work in the cover design and book layout.

To Sue Monk Kidd for the generous lessons in writing at the Sophia Institute and to Carolyn Rivers for continuing to bring light to the deep south with the work of Sophia.

To Dr. Wayne Dyer, who said to me (never mind the other 2,000 people in the room): *"Don't die with your music in you!"*

To Bev, who gave me permission, and especially to my momma, Peggy "Dare" Sowers Darr, thanks for the pen-name and recipes.

ENDNOTES

□ ◇ □ ◇ □ ◇ □ ◇ □ ◇ □ ◇ □ ◇ □ ◇ □ ◇ □ ◇ □ ◇ □ ◇ □ ◇ □ ◇ □ ◇ □ ◇ □ ◇ □

1   Flagg, F., *Grits (Girl Raised in the South) Guide to Life*, Penguin Books, 2003.

2   McLean S., *Out on a Limb*, Bantam Books, 1984, pg 357.

3   Myss, C., *Archetype Cards Guidebook*, Hay House, 2003, pg 77.

4   Redfield, J., *The Celestine Prophecy: An Adventure*, Warner Books, 1993, pg 223.

5   Solara, *The Star Borne: A Remembrance for the Awakened Ones*, Star Borne Unltd, 1989

6   Campbell, J. *The Power of Myth*, Doubleday, 1988, pg 31-38.

7   The legend that Solomon possessed a seal ring on which the name of God was engraved and by means of which he controlled the demons is related at length in Git. 68a, b. This legend is especially developed by Arabic writers, who declare that the ring, on which was engraved "the Most Great Name of God," and which was given to Solomon from heaven, was partly brass and partly iron. With the brass part of the ring Solomon signed his written comments to the good denii, and with the iron part he signed his commends to the evil genii, or devils. The Arabic writers declare also that Solomon received four jewels from our different angels, and that he set them in one ring, so that he could control the four elements.   • taken from JewishEncyclopedia.com

8   The New Revised Bible, John 15:13

9   Schucman, Dr. Helen, Foundation for Inner Peace: A Course
    in Miracles: Text, Workbook for Students, Manual for Teachers.
    Penguin, 1996

10 The Akashic Records are the repository of all human experi-
    ence; past, present and future, a record of all events within the
    universe and are part of the Cosmic Mind
     · taken from www.ElevatedTherapy.com

READING DISCUSSION QUESTIONS

The notion that we all have our own hero's journey puts life in perspective. It helps us relate to stories like Mystic Grits and see the challenges, relationships, "mean" people, spiritual guides, and career circumstances that confront us in life as part of the labyrinth we learn to walk through on our way to realizing and embracing our truest nature.

This guide will serve to help you ask some questions of yourself, start some discussions with your friends, or simply consider what intrigued or touched you by recording your thoughts in a journal.

Questions:

• How does the guidance of Maw Maw Precious serve the unfolding of DJ?

• What is the importance of having a foundation of faith or a set of beliefs?

• How does DJ's relationship change with men and others as she seeks guidance? When did it occur to her that these relationships with men were mirrors and growth charts? How about your relationships with significant others? Hmmm?

• Is it possible that she really did see a spaceship probe and her grandmother at Hanging Rock State Park?

• What could young Precious possibly learn from daring to question those teachings in her early church experiences? What were the risks? How are these things related to or different than your own questions about faith?

· What have you learned from the regrets of how you've approached those you lead (and we all do lead others at some point) and how you are different as a result of making a colossal mistake?

· What gives your life meaning?

· What have your children—or other children you encounter—come to teach you? What lessons are to be learned from the child within you?

· What can you imagine we might do with the other 90% of our brain or awaken in our "minds" if we learned to consciously and collectively access it? What could you dream up as a potential for creation? How do you really think we came to live on this planet?

· Who is God in this book? How do you know? What if there really is a God and He has a God?

· What will your best friend say about the impact you've had on her/his life?

· Why are you here?

To engage in a larger, world-wide discussion, go to the website and enter your comments on www.mysticgrits.com

ABOUT THE AUTHOR

A student of the heroine's journey, Darelyn **DJ** Mitsch has lived her life with one foot in the world of Spirit and one firmly planted in the world of Business—with a quiet mission to blend these often disparate worlds when coaching leaders around the world. As an entrepreneur, DJ focuses on integrated leadership, blending ancient wisdom with new technologies to more significantly engage employees for extraordinary results. In 1994, DJ founded The Pyramid Resource Group, the first Corporate Coaching Company in the US, with her life and business partner Barry Mitsch. She calls her team of amazing professional coaches, "angels with their wings tucked in." As a recognized leader in the coaching profession, DJ became a Master Certified Coach in 1998, one of the first 25 designated by the International Coach Federation (ICF) and then President of the ICF in 2001 where she helped build chapter programs around the globe. She has authored business books and a children's book of affirmations. This is her first book in the realm of "meta-fiction." DJ is the mother of two and resides in North Carolina with her family, where she is most at home with her southern accent and cheese grits.

COLOPHON

□ ◇ □ ◇ □ ◇ □ ◇ □ ◇ □ ◇ □ ◇ □ ◇ □ ◇ □ ◇ □ ◇ □ ◇ □ ◇ □ ◇ □ ◇ □ ◇ □ ◇ □ ◇ □ ◇ □

Intentionally, Mystic Grits was branded and typeset using two typeface families designed by women.

The Mystic Grits logo, title page, and header are set in award-winning, Odile, designed by Sibylle Hagmann in 2006.

The body of this work is set using Zuzana Licko's new type metamorphosis, Mrs Eaves XL, which was released in 2009. It is paired with her classic, 1996 version of Mrs Eaves. The typeface's name comes from Sarah Eaves, the lover of famed type designer John Baskerville. The classic Mrs Eaves face, and its beautiful ligatures are used in the sectional & chapter headers, along with Maw Maw's voice in the diary entries.

DJ's diary entries are typeset in Freehand 591 designed by Vincent Pacella.

Made in the USA